WALKING ROMAN ROADS IN LONSDALE
AND THE EDEN VALLEY

Fragment of a Roman carved stone built into the wall of a barn on the east side of the A683 just north of the entrance to Burrow Hall.

Walking Roman Roads in Lonsdale And The Eden Valley

By Philip Graystone S.M., M.A

Centre for North-West Regional Studies
University of Lancaster
2002
Series Editor: Jean Turnbull

Walking Roman Roads in Lonsdale and the Eden Valley

This volume is the 48th in a series published by the
Centre for North-West Regional Studies at the University of Lancaster.

Text copyright © Philip Graystone 2002

Designed, typeset, printed and bound by
JW Arrowsmith Ltd, Bristol

British Library Cataloguing-in-Publication Data
A catalogue record for this book is available from the British Library

ISBN No: 1–86220–123–4

Table of Contents

List of Sketch Maps

List of Photographs

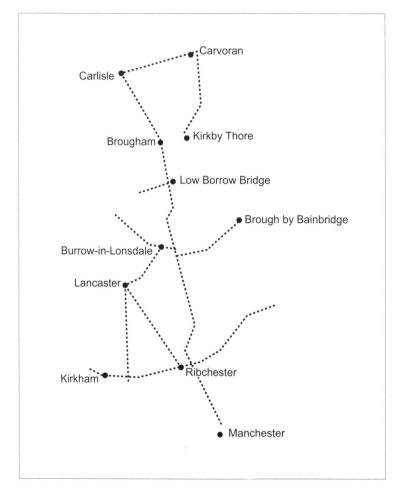

Sketch Map 1: Roman roads surveyed in this and preceding volumes of the series on walking Roman roads in North-West England (not to scale).

Introduction

This is the fourth volume in a series of studies designed to cover the network of Roman roads in north-west England (excluding the Lake District). The first, *Walking Roman Roads in Bowland*, was published in 1992; the second *Walking Roman Roads in East Cumbria* appeared in 1994, and the third *Walking Roman Roads in the Fylde and the Ribble Valley* in 1996. Readers who possess the earlier volumes will probably wish to omit these brief introductory remarks, since most of them have appeared, in substance at any rate, in previous introductions, but new readers may appreciate them.

Roman roads are perhaps the most substantial, the most widespread and certainly among the best known, of the many traces left by the Romans during the four centuries when this country formed part of their far-flung empire. Many people feel a thrill at travelling a stretch of road first laid out by Roman engineers nearly 2000 years ago, even when this stretch is now no more than a rigidly straight portion of modern motorway. Far more interesting are those lengths unaffected (one might almost say, unspoilt) by modernisation, and represented now by minor roads or footpaths or simply lines of hedgerows. Such stretches abound in north-west England, and it is not surprising that they form a magnet for people who enjoy a walk with an archaeological flavour.

While this study is primarily intended for such active amateurs, I have tried to make it as accurate as possible. This has entailed many hours of research in the proceedings of the various antiquarian societies of the area. It might be mentioned that these very often record the investigations and observations of non-professionals as far as Roman roads (as distinct from forts, settlements etc) are concerned, confirming that knowledge of the existence and present condition of Roman routes owes much to exploration by interested amateurs. Also that browsing through these records can often be almost as fascinating as striding the roads themselves.

A secondary objective of this brief volume and its companions – perhaps not originally intended but increasingly adopted in the light of experience – is to record the state of the Roman roads in the north west at the close of the millennium. The picture is constantly changing. On the one hand modern farming techniques – for example deep ploughing and field enlargement, often involving hedge destruction – have frequently obscured traces of Roman roads. On the other hand the construction of new roads, especially the recent development of motorways in Lancashire, has obliterated whole tracts. It is only too likely that this process will continue, hence the importance of recording the state of play, so to speak, at frequent intervals.

The centrepiece of this series of books was originally meant to be the Roman road from Ribchester to Carlisle by way of Burrow-in-Lonsdale, Low Borrow Bridge and Brougham, this being the generally accepted main Roman route to the north, west of the Pennines – road number 7 in Margary's classification (Margary 1957). The road actually commenced, not at Ribchester but further south, in (modern) Manchester (Margary, suggested Chester, but recent work in Manchester would modify this – see the sketch map on page 56 which shows the northern main road branching from the transpennine Chester/York road). The omission of the section from Manchester to Ribchester from the original plan for these four volumes was not thought serious, since this stretch, to a great extent, passes through urban surroundings where all visible traces are obliterated and which are certainly not walking territory.

However, in researching for, and writing, these books, I have become more and more strongly convinced that the road from Manchester to Carlisle should be considered as a single unit, even if it was not originally planned and constructed as such. Certainly the first two sections, Manchester/Ribchester and Ribchester/Burrow-in-Lonsdale are not discontinuous; the alignment of the first section extends beyond Ribchester (which it by-passes) to a point over three miles north of the Ribble. The situation at Burrow-in-Lonsdale implies even less discontinuity; once again the fort itself is bypassed, this time at a greater distance, and the alignment is uninterrupted.

The upshot of all this is that I would feel this group of studies to be incomplete if it did not take note of the southernmost section of the main road – the section from Manchester to Ribchester – and since this was omitted from the first volume (where it would have fitted best), and in subsequent volumes, it should at least be included as an appendix to this fourth volume. I am well aware that this will appear illogical and clumsy, and apologise accordingly. Moreover this section, as already mentioned, traverses, at least for the first few miles, urban and suburban districts where there is little or nothing of interest visible and where walking is not the most attractive of pursuits. Even so, the section beyond Tottington and Edgeworth, where the road emerges on to the moors and crosses difficult country, is certainly not without interest, and the final stretch across the Ribble valley is well worth detailed investigation.

Furthermore, points of interest do arise even in tracing Roman routes through modern urbanised areas. For instance, the particular road considered here is followed very closely by Bury New Road throughout its urban length. Margary points out that Bury New Road is a turnpike construction and opines that it was probably laid out along a path or bridleway which succeeded the Roman road. It would be interesting to have confirmation of this, also to find out about possible discoveries in the course of laying out the turnpike and about possible reuse of Roman material as metalling.

Some further explanation is called for regarding parts of the main body of the work – the road north of Burrow-in-Lonsdale and its branch roads.

Section Four, for example, which sees the main road arriving at Low Borrow Bridge, moves away for a few pages from the road itself and looks around at the environs of the Roman fort. In particular it has something to say, by way of description and illustration, about the aqueduct which supplied the fort and remains a well-preserved and spectacular relic. The only explanation I can offer is my own fascination with this area of Roman Britain – remote and unexplored for centuries, and now traversed by a main rail link and by the roaring traffic of the frantically busy M6.

The reader will also doubtless note the extra attention given, in Section Eleven, to the branch road which led south-westwards, across Whinfell, from this same fort of Low Borrow Bridge. This is a road about which little seems to have been recorded, but in its early stages it is one of the most interesting I have ever encountered. I hope the extra pictures I have included will help to explain this. It is a pity that so little has so far been discovered about the later sections of this route.

The advice about maps given in previous volumes is so important that I reproduce it yet again here. The maps accompanying the text are only rough sketches, intended, not for navigation, but to give some idea of the whereabouts of the various photographs. For navigation purposes the reader will need to arm himself/herself with the excellent series of Ordnance Survey (O.S.) Pathfinder (1: 25000) maps of this area, to which constant reference is made in the text and which are, indeed, quite indispensable for the serious student of the Roman Roads. The serial numbers of the maps required for each area are printed below the title of the relevant section. To acquire all these maps will represent a rather formidable outlay, but one which is well worthwhile in terms of usefulness and adding to the enjoyment of the exploration. For absolute completeness O.S. Outdoor Leisure maps no. 5 and 7 – English Lakes North Eastern and South Eastern Areas – would be needed, but the areas involved are small and the extra expense might not seem worthwhile. The one-inch O.S. Landranger maps – serial numbers also displayed – offer a more economical alternative, but a far less satisfactory one in terms of information and guidance. This is especially important when using this present volume, since for the first time and in answer to various promptings, I have included occasional map grid references in the text; these are based on the Pathfinder maps.

Once again notes on access are given at the end of each section. Many derelict Roman roads are either accompanied by rights of way or can be viewed from publicly accessible points; where this is not so permission should, of course, be sought.

References to literary sources are given when appropriate, so that the reader may seek further information on points of particular interest. In the body of the text these references are given in abbreviated form; the bibliography on page 70 contains fuller details.

I am indebted once again to Dr. David Shotter, who provides a fitting finale in the form of another scholarly essay, this time on Roman Carlisle. It is appropriate that his contribution should form the epilogue to this book, since it was owing to his advice and encouragement that this group of studies was first commenced; moreover Carlisle is the northern destination of the principal Roman road in the north west and in this series. Finally, my thanks to all those good people who welcomed me and gave me help and advice during my journeys of exploration, especially, yet again, to my constant companions, Barbara and Miles Sharratt.

Philip Graystone
October 2001

Part One: The Roman Road from Burrow-in-Lonsdale to Carlisle

Section One

The crossing of Leck Beck; along Wandales Lane

(Landranger 97; Pathfinder 628)

The course of the main Roman road to the north, running west of the Pennines, from Ribchester northwards to Burrow-in-Lonsdale, has been described in a previous volume (Graystone, 1992). It will be recalled that this section traverses nearly 30 miles of difficult and hilly country between the two forts. Because of the distance, it has been suggested that there was an intermediate station, but none has so far been found. Like Ribchester, Burrow-in-Lonsdale is about a mile to the west of the road. Both forts are situated on the banks of the stream crossed by the road; in the case of Ribchester this is the Ribble, in the case of Burrow, the Leck Beck; the south bank of this stream forms the northern boundary of the survey in the previous volume.

Before investigating the actual crossing of the Leck Beck, it would be as well to look at one final feature of the stretch, south of the beck, which has not hitherto been described, but which the enthusiast will certainly not want to miss. This is the base of what is almost certainly a Roman milestone, still standing in its original roadside position. It is found just beyond the northern end of the straight track carrying the Roman line almost due north from Crowder Farm and beyond. This track meets the modern by-road from Cowan Bridge to Overtown at a point where this by-road makes a sharp right-angled bend, which brings it on to the Roman line for a short distance before it slants off westwards. It is alongside this short stretch that the stone stands, on the eastern side of the road, about 25 yards north of the end of the aforementioned track (map ref. 630761). It is quite hard to find, being set right against the roadside wall, hidden by vegetation and covered with moss, and, because of this, difficult to photograph successfully (as is evident from the picture on page 2). In its present state it is about two feet high, with an irregular upper surface suggesting that the top part has been broken off. Its position, size, and typical cylindrical shape render its identification practically certain (Charlesworth,1965). The stone now serves as a boundary marker, with "Leck" inscribed on its south side and "B" (for Burrow?) on its north side; there is no visible trace of any earlier inscription.

It is worth mentioning that the stone is just under one (Roman) mile east of the fort of Burrow-in-Lonsdale and could conceivably have

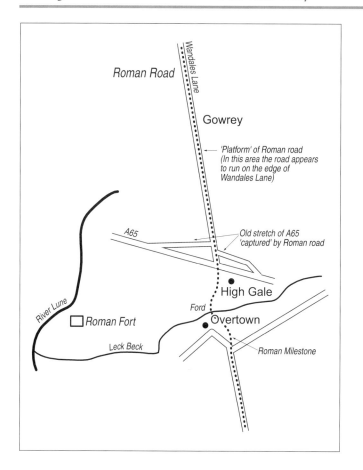

Sketch Map 2: The Roman Road in the Leck Beck area.

Figure 1: The base of the probable Roman milestone (on the eastern edge of the Roman road).

measured the distance along a side road to the fort, which is strategically placed between the Leck Beck and the river Lune, near the point where the one meets the other. There must have been a connecting road between road and fort, but this does not appear to have survived. It is true that a footpath, with right of way, makes the connection, but this is hardly direct enough to represent a Roman road.

Not far north of the stone the formidable obstacle of the Leck Beck is encountered. In spite of its name, the beck is a substantial stream, equivalent to any river, especially after a rainy spell. Its banks, moreover, are high and steep, so that it would present quite a problem to the road builders. Hence the Roman crossing point will certainly have left visible traces. There are, however, no evident signs on the actual main alignment, which is not in doubt at this point, pursuing a straight and well-defined line almost due north and south for several miles on both sides of the Beck. Consequently one looks for the diversion which is so often met with at stream crossings. A short distance downstream from the Roman line the steep banks on each side have been hollowed out to approach a ford, which has evidently still been in use until recent times (See picture below). Nowadays it is replaced by a footbridge at the same point (629764). The short approach lane to the ford from the south side points directly back to the northern end of the lane marking the Roman road south of Overtown. Hence it is highly likely that this ford represents the Roman crossing point, especially since there is no sign of any alternative.

It should, however, be noted that there are no visible remains of any linking stretch on the north side of the beck; when traces again appear, at High Gale, about 400 yards north of the beck, they are on exactly the same alignment – almost due north-south – as was maintained for over three miles on the south side of the beck.

I am indebted to the kindness and courtesy of John and Anne Kerr of High Gale Farm for permission to explore the interesting stretch north

Figure 2: The site of the old ford across the Leck Beck alongside the modern footbridge.

of the beck. The line of the road appears quite plainly emerging from a gate in the south wall of the field west of the farm buildings; it then crosses this field as a broken ridge, not substantial but nevertheless quite distinct. Before reaching the north wall of the field it has to cross a small stream called Eller Beck; the crossing point is marked by an abutment on the south bank. Much stone outcrops here – indeed a line of stone on the east of the mound is suggestive of a kerb. There is a break in the bank on the oppo-site (north) bank of the beck. Northwards a small wood intervenes; after this the line appears to be marked by a level strip of ground at the bottom of the hillside, and then by a low grassy ridge immediately to the west of the path to High Gale, which swings alongside it at this point.

At the northern end of this path the line of the Roman road is con-tinued for about ¼ mile by a section of the old (now disused) A65. This is an interesting case (possibly clearer on the map than on the ground) of the 'capture' of a stretch of later road as it crosses a Roman line, a phe-nomenon, surprisingly common, which will be familiar to all experienced Roman road enthusiasts. No doubt it has its origin in the widespread use, by our ancestors, of Roman roads as boundaries; the later road, instead of crossing the boundary directly, would run along it until it ceased or until a convenient crossing point was reached. In this case the A65 has recently been straightened to avoid the awkward deviation so caused.

When the old A65 swings away to the west, at Kirby Lonsdale station, the line is continued for the next one-and-a-half miles by a minor road known as Wandales Lane, gradually moving slightly west of the rigid northerly line hitherto followed. Percival Ross, who in the early years of the twentieth century was so assiduous in tracing the Roman routes of north-western England, describes the Roman road as lying just to the east of Wandales Lane as it leaves the station and approaches Gowrey farm, not far to the north. Following his directions, on my last visit, passing the second field south of the farm (630777), I looked over the wall bound-ing the lane on the east side, and there, just as he described it, was the "road platform" with a water-filled ditch on its further side.

This continued for perhaps 200 yards. North of the farm, according to Ross, Wandales Lane merges with the actual course of the road itself (Ross, 1916). This section of the Wandales Lane is narrow, straight, and rather featureless, like many present-day roads which follow a Roman line. Roman roads did not attract later settlers because, the Romans, being pre-occupied with rapid and economical communication, tended to by-pass amenities like springs, which would be needed for habitation sites. In this case Casterton (a name suggestive of a Roman site, though I have never heard of any discoveries there) and, further north, Barbon, are noticeably just off the line. The other point to notice is the proximity of the Lune; the Roman road is set to follow the river on its journey north and for the next 20 miles will never be more than a mile away from it.

As the road goes north, beyond Gowrey, it passes, about a mile away to the east, an extensive scatter of early settlements and field systems (the settle-ments are noted on the Pathfinder map) covering quite a wide area. Trial

Figure 3: The 'road platform' on the east side of Wandales Lane.

excavation (Lowndes, 1964) has indicated a date within the Roman period for some of these, and the lay-out of the complex indicates cultivation rather than stock-rearing. This is interesting, since the land, on limestone above the valley, is not first-grade arable country. Very likely the cultivation extended westwards on to the valley floor, where later ploughing will have removed traces, but the inclusion also of the marginal land indicates a strong demand for its products in the Roman era, presumably to supply the neighbouring fort at Burrow-in-Lonsdale. Trackways must have connected the area with the main Roman road which we are following.

Wandales lane moves westwards, off the Roman line, at a point marked by a junction (628799) where minor roads lead west to Casterton and east to Langthwaite (the O.S. Pathfinder map – in this case 628 – is indispensable here as elsewhere). This is the sort of place where one looks for traces; I have seen a hump on the line in the near corner of the next field to the north. It is also a convenient break point in our survey.

Note on access
Both banks of the Leck Beck (and in particular the old ford) are accessible by footpaths with right of way. The disused section of the A65, and of course Wandales Lane, are also accessible, and being minor roads can be walked without too much difficulty.

Section Two

Barbon and Middleton

(Landranger 97; Pathfinders 628, 617)

For just under half a mile after the break point at the end of the last section, Wandales lane follows a northerly course never more than 150 yards west of the Roman line, and about halfway along this stretch a track, with right of way, leaves the lane going eastwards to Hole House; actually the track has now been surfaced to make a drive. After a short distance this drive crosses the Roman line (at 628803), and looking northwards through a convenient gap in the hedge at this point, a very distinct ridge is seen in the second field to the north, with a solitary tree on its western edge and a growth of reeds or rough grass on its eastern edge. A section was dug across this stretch in 1958, and the road was found in a good state of preservation. It was built on a foundation layer of brush-wood, possibly because of the wet nature of the land at this point. Above this was a layer of large river cobbles, and above this again a layer of tightly packed gravel and small stones (Ewbank, 1960).

Returning to Wandales Lane (or its continuation) and following this north for about 300 yards, one reaches the point where the lane swings east by a right-angled bend and heads off to Fell Garth. Just east of the bend the Roman line is again crossed, and the damaged ridge can be seen, though not very plainly, in the field to the south. Wandales Lane does not return to the line, which for most of the next mile or so is free of modern roads. About a fifth of a mile further on, just south of a small triangular wood, the line of the Roman road passes close to a standing stone (627810), marked on the map as 'Cross Stone' (and pictured on page 7). Before reaching this, the course of the Roman road in the field to the south appears to be marked by an overgrown ridge which divides the fields and has a line of trees along it.

The Cross Stone has an incised cruciform mark carved on it and stands close by the course of the road, traces of which are not readily seen here. Such wayside crosses are generally a sign of age in a road, and hence not infrequently are found alongside Roman roads. Immediately north of the cross the line passes through the triangular wood aforementioned. Eighty years ago Ross saw traces in the wood, not now visible to me. However he notes also two large trees marking the course onwards to the drive to Whelprigg, and these are still standing. The stream which flows east-west just north of the drive must have been crossed by the road very near the present lodge (Ross, 1916).

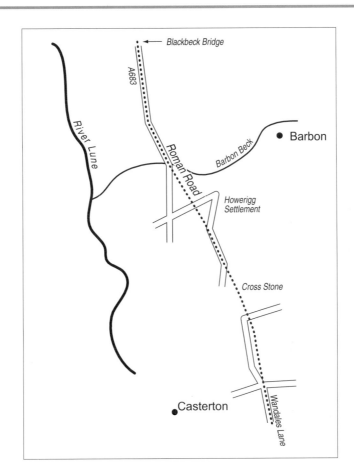

Sketch Map 3: The Roman Road between Casterton and Barbon (not to scale).

Figure 4: The 'Cross Stone' which stands alongside the line of the Roman Road near Whelprigg.

Figure 5: The overgrown ridge marking the course of the Roman road south of the field where the Cross Stone stands.

Just beyond this stream, after crossing the disused railway, the Roman road is followed by the present by-road for about 400 yards. The modern road then slants away to the east, and the Roman road, now heading distinctly west of north, crosses a field in which are the traces of an ancient settlement marked on the Pathfinder map (at 625819) and known to archaeologists as the Howerigg settlement (from a nearby farm of that name). This appears to the uninitiated observer as a series of irregularities in the field lying in the angle between the (modern) road we have been following and Scaleber Lane which crosses it here. On closer and more skilled examination, it is revealed as a series of mainly rectangular enclosures within a perimeter embankment. This feature evidently overlies the Roman road, which has led archaeologists to regard it, tentatively, as post-Roman in date (Lowndes, 1963).

The Roman line now crosses Scaleber Lane, and is marked by field boundaries, and intermittently by trees, for most of the distance to the A683, which it reaches in about one-third of a mile (at 623825). Slanting across the A683 at this point it crosses Barbon Beck just west of the bridge which takes the A683 across, called on the Pathfinder map 'Hodge Bridge'. Looking down from this bridge, the Roman crossing point seems to be marked by a very substantial paved ford in the river bed. It is not, of course, claimed that this is Roman; it has every appearance of being a relatively recent construction; but it may well be the successor to an earlier ford. There is, however, no indication of an approach in either bank; possibly the construction of the modern bridge has obliterated such traces.

After crossing the beck the Roman road coincides with the A683, and indeed follows it approximately for the next four/five miles. Its course, as earlier indicated, is dictated by that of the Lune, always near at hand on the west side. Since the general course of the river bends from just west of north to just east of north over this five mile stretch, the course of the

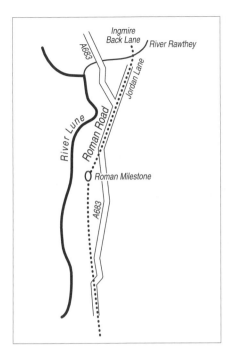

Roman road (and of the A683) does the same. The Roman road, as usually happens, has a more direct alignment (or series of alignments) than its modern successor, and hence its course can sometimes be detected within the slight deviations of the A683.

The enthusiast who has followed this splendid Roman road northwards from Ribchester will realise that the section we are now considering is virtually the first instance in which it coincides with a modern main road for any considerable distance. Hence following it on foot becomes, for these few miles, rather more tiresome, and furthermore physical traces are entirely obliterated. It is worth, however, noticing (as we did in the last section) the absence of villages or even hamlets, even where the Roman route is followed, as here, by an A-class modern road.

The rough sketch map on page 7 shows this stretch up to Blackbeck Bridge, but as always the Pathfinder – still No. 628 – is required for the details. From this it can be seen that, apart from a very slight diversion just north of Blackbeck Bridge, the A683 follows the Roman line closely

Figure 6: The Roman milestone at Middleton; the trees in the background mark the River Lune.

for the first mile or so. A quarter of a mile further on the modern road swings to the east, bypassing – as Percy Ross noted 80 years ago – a knoll about 340 feet high, over the shoulder of which the Roman road goes. He was, of course, writing at a time when such details could be observed at leisure; nowadays the frequency and speed of modern traffic makes observation on a main road like this difficult and hazardous. Ross indicates that the A683 rejoins the line about a quarter of a mile further on, and the Pathfinder map follows him in this, but there are reasons for believing that the diversion is a good deal longer, and that the Roman road ran closer to the river for perhaps a mile (Ross, 1916).

At any rate this is certainly the case about half a mile further on, where the A683 passes Middleton House on its eastern side and the lane to Abbey Farm on the west. About 300 yards north of this point, and perhaps 100 yards west of the A683, a fine Roman milestone stands in the field (at 623859). It can be seen from the modern road, but is not immediately accessible. However it stands adjacent to a track leading to Hawking Hall, which though not a right of way at this point, becomes one as it approaches the Hall.

The milestone was found buried in the ground a short distance from its present location – nearer to the river, in fact. Since crop marks have indicated that the Roman road also ran closer to the river hereabouts, it seems that the find spot of the stone was at, or near to, its original position. The stone carries a twofold inscription – the upper one is the original Roman lettering and reads 'M P LIII' (= Millia Passuum LIII, i.e. 53 Roman miles). (The lower inscription, also in Latin, records the nineteenth century discovery and re-erection of the stone). Fifty three Roman miles is an accurate measure of the distance from Carlisle via this road, and important conclusions have been drawn from the inscription.

Figure 7: Another view of the Roman milestone at Middleton. The M of the Roman inscription is just visible.

A tribe called the Carvetii, with its administrative centre at Carlisle, is thought to be recorded in this part of the Upper Lune Valley, and this inscription could be an indication that the territory of this tribe included this area. Alternatively – and this is independent of the inscription – it has been suggested that a milestone such as this might have been erected to mark the boundaries (of patrol etc) of the areas controlled by neighbouring forts – in this case Burrow-in-Lonsdale to the south and Low Borrow Bridge to the north (Birley, 1953).

After crossing Stockdale Beck the A683 swings to a direction east of north, and again runs on or near to the Roman alignment, which hereabouts alters course towards the east in order to keep roughly parallel with the river. At Middleton Hall Bridge, however, the modern road bears west and for almost half a mile leaves the Roman line, which continues straight ahead, accompanied for some way by field boundaries. It is rejoined by the A683 beyond a (disused) railway bridge and is then followed by it very closely for about three-quarters of a mile. When the A683 finally leaves the line, and heads off to the west to cross the Lune at Middleton Bridge, the Roman road continues to be marked by a narrow by-road called Jordan Lane – rigidly straight for just under a mile, until it is diverted at the crossing of the (disused) railway which has never been far away for the last few miles. (Pathfinder no. 617 commences just north of this crossing). If this straight alignment is continued, it will reach the River Rawthey, in about 1500 yards, at a place (638911) where the river bends and broadens – a suitable place for a ford, by its present appearance.

On the opposite, north, bank, which is quite steep, there are traces of a terrace slanting up to the west, and within a short distance Ingmire Back Lane takes up the line in a more northerly direction in keeping with the known course subsequently followed. The lane is not rigidly straight, but nevertheless direct; the route is now entering more difficult country where bends are to be expected.

Figure 8: Possible position of the Roman ford across the River Rawthey on the line of the road, looking south.

Note on access

Wandales Lane is, of course, a public road, albeit a minor one, and the drive to Hole House is a right of way, from which the ridge of the Roman road to the north is easily viewed. The Cross Stone, though quite near to the road, is not actually accessible by public footpath; on my visit the people at the lodge on Whelprigg drive readily gave me leave to view this interesting monument and the adjacent traces of the road, as described in the text.

The ancient settlement (known as Howerigg Settlement after the name of a nearby farm) lies between the (present) road and Scaleber Lane and is visible from the present road. As indicated in the text, the fine Roman milestone at Middleton is not actually on a point of public access, but is within a short distance of the path, with right of way, which leads south-westwards from the wayside church at Middleton. Jordan Lane is a very narrow public by-road, and the suggested site of the ford across the Rawthey can be viewed from the north bank by following the path, with right of way, from the A683 to Brigflatts. Most of Ingmire Back Lane is public right of way.

Section Three

Approaching Low Borrow Bridge

(Landranger 97; Pathfinder 617 & 607)

After about half a mile, Ingmire Back Lane reaches Ingmire Hall, on the A684, and here commences one of the few sections in which the course of the Roman road (albeit for only a short distance) has not been traced in detail, though its general direction is not in doubt. Margary follows Ross in stating that for the next three-quarters of a mile the road crosses the fields, presumably continuing the line of Ingmire Back Lane, that is, almost due north, though neither author identifies any visible traces, and none seem evident. Certainly this line would bring it to the junction of Slacks Lane and Howgill Lane (638932), north of Height of Winder Farm, and there is general agreement that the definite course northwards is clear from this point (Ross, 1916; Margary, 1957).

Indeed, for the next four miles, until the crossing of Carlingill Beck is reached, the Roman line is followed almost exactly by very minor modern roads; firstly by Howgill Lane and then by Fairmile Road. A glance at the Pathfinder map (no. 617) shows that the road is laid out on a single alignment, pointing just west of north, roughly parallel to the Lune and never very far from it. Within this alignment there are, perforce, local variations at the beck crossings – Chapel Beck, Fairmile Beck and Carlingill especially – but from New House northwards to Eel Gill – a distance of over three miles – the road is never more than 150 yards from its intended course; the skill shown by the engineers in keeping so close to their planned line in this very difficult terrain is most impressive. This is very evident if the Roman road is compared, on the Pathfinder map, with its modern counterpart, the B 6257, on the opposite (west) side of the Lune. Like the Roman road, this is obviously intended as a through north/south route along the Lune valley, but though remarkably direct, it is much less so than Howgill Lane and Fairmile Road. The curving route of the M6, which comes into the picture as the Tebay Gorge is approached, is of course influenced by other considerations.

Before considering the Roman road in detail, it is worth noting the place names that occur along it. Villages (apart from the scattered hamlet of Howgill) are absent throughout – a characteristic of roads following Roman routes which has already been remarked upon. But there are three farm names featuring the element 'gate' – Gate Side, Gate House and Fairmile Gate. Place names in this area are mainly of Norse origin, and the root word here is Old Norse 'gata', a road (Ekwall, 1960), indicating

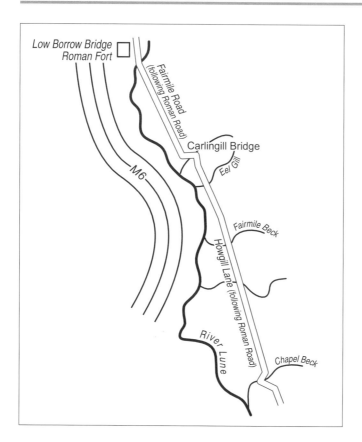

Sketch Map 5: The section south of Low Borrow Bridge (not to scale).

Figure 9: Looking south from Eel Gill along the Roman road (here followed by Fairmile Road) showing the typical position above and parallel to the Lune, on the right. Note the growth of coarse grass marking the ditches.

that the road was already in existence and still recognisable when the Norse settlement took place.

For the first three miles Howgill Lane is walled on both sides, making it difficult to observe such features as embankments or side ditches. But it is fairly clear that it is terraced along the hillside, which must have involved a fair amount of heavy work in moving earth and rock. The crossings of the various becks are of great interest, since there seems little reason to doubt that they represent in detail the original Roman plan; indeed, apart from the replacement of fords by bridges, practically the whole of this section is accepted as following the Roman line very closely (Ross, 1916; Codrington, 1918; Margary 1957). The valleys carved out by the becks are very steep-sided, necessitating well-constructed terraces and deep cuttings. This is especially evident at Chapel Beck, where the road bends sharply first west and then east to ease the steep gradient as the stream is approached from the south, and then repeats this zig-zag on the north bank before resuming its general alignment. The crossings, further north, of Fairmile and Carlingill Becks, show similar features.

(It is worth recalling that Margary observed 40 years ago that great care must be exercised in driving along the narrow Howgill Lane, especially at the beck crossings where the bends are sharp and the gradients steep; the advice still holds good; Margary, 1957).

North of Fairmile Beck the road (now Fairmile Road) loses its walls and emerges on to the open hillside. This makes it easier to observe the general directness of the road along this difficult hillside, and also to keep in view the river Lune – now close at hand on the west side – and the motorway and railway just beyond. The gradual narrowing of the Tebay gorge, and the consequent drawing together of all these avenues of communication, old and new, river, Roman road, railway and M6, is quite dramatic.

Figure 10: The crossing of Fairmile Beck, from the north. The bridge replaces an earlier ford, but the approaches, curving to ease the gradient, running through deep cuttings, and resuming the alignment on the south side, are probably original.

Just before reaching Carlingill, Fairmile Road deviates from the course of its Roman predecessor for a very short distance – perhaps 500 yards. The deviation, which commences just north of Eel Gill and rejoins the Roman line just short of Carlingill, shows up on the map as a slight bend westwards in the route, but is plainer still on the ground. The rerouted present road takes a lower level, whereas the Roman road goes straight on (northwards) over the shoulder of the hill, appearing as a rough bare ridge, especially at its northern end, with boulders outcropping here and there and with the metalling exposed by water action in places. In early summer, 1962, a section was cut across this stretch (at 625994) by members of the Sedgwick Society, Sedbergh School, under the direction of E.M.L. McAdam, who subsequently published the results. The section was cut towards the northern end of the stretch, and seems to have been left open after excavation, for it can still be seen as a trench around four/five feet wide and three feet deep running right across the ridge (a distance given by McAdam as 24 feet). There are some quite large boulders in and around the trench, evidently from the road foundations (McAdam, 1964).

North of this very interesting stretch comes the crossing of Carlingill Beck, negotiated by a V-shaped deviation upstream leading to the present bridge. This has evidently replaced an earlier ford; the damaged terraces which gave access to it are apparent on both sides of the beck just upstream from the bridge.

Immediately after passing Carlingill Beck the Roman road takes up a new alignment, more west of north, which brings it, in a gradual slant down the valley side, to its crossing point at Salterwath bridge on the Lune. This is another significant name – 'wath' is an old Norse word for ford, and the implication that this ford was in use by salt-carriers is a clear indication of antiquity.

Figure 11: The north face of the McAdam trench, with the ridge of the Roman road beyond. The modern road can be seen on the left.

Figure 12: Another view of the McAdam trench, looking along the trench from its eastern end.

Thus the Roman road finds itself on the west side of the Lune for the remainder of the length of the Tebay gorge, after following the east bank since arriving in the Lune valley at Burrow-in-Lonsdale. Fortunately the modern avenues of communication – the railway and the M6 – have kept to the west bank throughout, making possible the survival of the very interesting section of Roman road which has been studied in this section.

Note on access
Since the Roman road virtually coincides almost throughout this section with minor roads still in use (Howgill Lane and Fairmile Road) there is no difficulty about access. However a word of warning might be appreciated by intending drivers – these roads are very narrow, and at the beck crossings gradients are very steep and bends sharp. Furthermore it is not always easy to find parking places when required, though it is worth looking for them, since the enthusiast will certainly wish to explore the more interesting stretches on foot.

Among the features to look out for – rather surprising in this remote landscape – are the occasional traces left by small farming communities, active, it is generally thought, in the Roman period. These lie mainly east of the road (to the west, towards the valley floor, they may well have been ploughed out). They consist mainly of banks and ditches, and are not easy for the amateur to interpret. But the settlement at Low Carlingill, for example, has left traces that are highly visible. Such farmsteads must have depended greatly on the nearby fort of Low Borrow Bridge as a market for their produce (Higham and Jones, 1985).

Section Four

Low Borrow Bridge

(Landranger no. 91; Pathfinder no. 607)

About a quarter of a mile north-west of the Lune crossing at Salterwath Bridge, Fairmile Road (or its continuation) passes the site of the Roman fort of Low Borrow Bridge. The present road at this point probably represents, at least approximately, the course of its Roman predecessor, which appears to have by-passed the fort, to which no doubt side roads gave access, in much the same way as our modern main roads tend to by-pass the centres of population which they serve. The fort platform is just north of the farm buildings which now share the site, and on my last visit the good lady at the farm kindly invited me to make a closer inspection. The remains of the fort are still impressively evident, not in the shape of walls or buildings still standing, but in the shape of the surrounding rampart, mounds and ditches, especially on the west side (the forts is orientated almost exactly to the four cardinal compass points).

It is intriguing to find a Roman fort with such visible traces within a few yards of a modern motorway (the M6 and the main railway line run close by the north-western angle). Yet the sight of the mountains all around reminds one that its situation must have been very remote indeed before the coming of these modern means of communication.

Figure 13: The south-west corner of the ramparts of the Roman fort of Low Borrow Bridge. Faint traces of the ditches are visible, on the site if not in the picture.

An even better overall impression of the fort can be gained from the main road – the A685 – on the west side of the motorway. There is a convenient lay-by on the A685 (at 608007) just north of House Bridge, where the explorer can leave his/her car in order to walk southwards up the hill. Great care is needed – traffic is frequent and fast and it is not easy always to take evasive action by walking alongside the road instead of on it. But 300 or 400 yards further along, a marvellous view unfolds of the fort and its setting. Looking back, in a north-easterly direction, across the M6 and the railway, the near-rectangular fort platform and its ramparts stand out with remarkable clarity alongside the farm buildings. The juxtaposition of old and new – the Roman fort and the ultra-modern motorway – in the spectacular setting of the Tebay gorge, make this a view well worth stopping for.

From this same point, looking westwards up the hill on the west side of the A685, the sharp-eyed enthusiast might be able to make out one of the most fascinating features of this very remarkable landscape – the aqueduct which the Romans dug, slanting down the hillside of Birk Knott, to serve their fort of Low Borrow Bridge. It is worth asking permission to explore this feature more closely. It is fed by a waterfall high on the hillside, and then descends on an even gradient, still carrying water for much of its length, and clearly marked by a growth of reeds and long grass even where it is now dry. It is a real thrill to stand alongside this watercourse and follow it with the eye north-eastwards directly down to the rectangle of the fort, standing out clearly alongside the farm buildings in the valley below, across the busy motorway and the railway. There can be few more complete examples of a Roman aqueduct in the country; J.W. Anstee's description will certainly of interest to people who cannot examine it more closely (Anstee, 1975).

Another interesting adjunct to the fort – though not now visible – is the cemetery, which was discovered 300 yards south of the fort during pipelaying in 1991. Both inhumations and cremation urns were present, together with one complete tombstone, commemorating Aelia Sentica, wife of Aurelius Verulus (Lambert, 1996). It has been suggested that the civilian settlement, a characteristic of practically all Roman forts, lay between the cemetery and the southern rampart (Shotter and White, 1995).

Before the advent of the M6, the (Roman) road we have been following, from Carlingill, after crossing the Lune and passing the fort, joined the A685 in a way which suggested that this latter road now took up the Roman line. Nowadays the junction has been much altered by the building of the motorway. However, north of the junction, it remains very probable that the Roman road is in fact continued in direction by the A685, which follows a fairly straight course parallel to the Lune for the next mile. Ross believed that the Roman line continues to be indicated by the A685 where this bends east to cross the river at Lune's Bridge, but Martin Allan has argued persuasively that this would involve the Roman engineers in needless crossing and recrossing of the river, and has postulated a route which would keep the Roman road west of the Lune on a line which would

Figure 14: Looking upwards along the higher reaches of the aqueduct channel, close to the summit of the fell.

Figure 15: Further down, the aqueduct still carries water as it slants down the hill.

Figure 16: This picture shows the lowest reaches of the aqueduct, pointing directly to the fort, which stands out as a raised rectangular platform to the left of the farm buildings. Also visible is the Roman road from the south marked by the line of trees sloping down the hill and passing close by the fort.

take it close by Loupsfell Farm. This would certainly fit in well with the next very definite traces of the road, which are found south of the Tebay service area on the motorway (Ross, 1916; Allan, 1984).

Note on access

It is unfortunate that, apart from the road lengths followed by modern roads, none of the interesting features noted in this section – fort site, aqueduct, and Martin Allan's postulated route over Loupsfell – are accessible without permission, which the enthusiast will certainly wish to request.

Section Five

North of Tebay

(Landranger 91, 90; Pathfinder 607, 597)

The construction of the M6 motorway through the Tebay gorge, though it unfortunately obliterated traces of the Roman road in the area under consideration, yet brought about a fascinating juxtaposition of the ancient and ultra-modern. Examples of this have already been noted further south, where the M6 ran almost side by side with Howgill Lane, and in the vicinity of the fort itself at Low Borrow Bridge. But the most spectacular instance is at the Tebay Service Station, where the motorway and the Roman road literally and visibly come together. On the pathfinder map (607) a field wall is seen approaching what the map calls 'Tebay West Services' from a direction just east of south; (a footpath marked 'Roman Road' north of the M6, which is crossed obliquely here by our road, continues precisely the same line). On the ground traces are plainer still, for looking south from the southern boundary of the service area, at the point (607061) where the path leads off to the sewerage works, the wall shown on the map is clearly seen descending the hillside opposite. It evidently follows the line of the eastern ditch of the Roman road; the western ditch runs on a parallel course a few yards away, with the road ridge in between, as is clear from the photograph alongside the sketch map.

Within the service area itself, a wood lies along the east side of the car park, and just inside this wood is a steep bank (the result of levelling for the car park?) along the top of which the Roman ridge apparently continues on the same line (west of north) as before. It is seen in great strength among the trees as it approaches the motorway at the north end of the wood, with ditches clearly showing.

North of the M6 a field boundary immediately takes up the line from a point just north of the bridge which takes the side road to Orton across the motorway. It is evident that the construction of the latter, with its wide spacing at this point between its north and south carriageways, must have destroyed many traces of the Roman road along a stretch that Percival Ross describes as the 'finest piece of Roman road in Westmorland' (Ross, 1920). However further traces are met with in spectacular fashion in the rough pasture to the north, as Sproat Ghyll farm is approached (around 604072), with ditches sometimes three to four feet deep and with a well-marked ridge between on which the metalling sometimes outcrops, especially where there has been a wash-out.

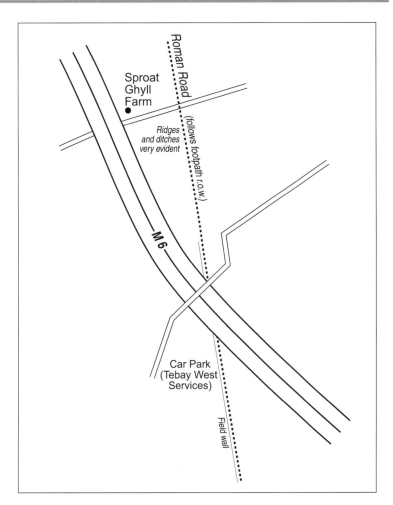

Sketch Map 6: The Roman Road in the Sproat Ghyll area north of Tebay (not to scale).

Figure 17: Looking south along the Roman road descending the hillside south of Tebay motorway service area: wall and ditch on the east side, ditch on the west.

The many large rocks on this field, especially along the course of the road (were they levered out during construction?) indicate that the land has never been ploughed. It formed part of Orton Low Moor before the advent of the motorway, and the remains now surviving are only the remnant of the more extensive traces which, according to Margary, were formerly seen. Even now they are very impressive, especially in the very unusual depth of the ditches. Ross accounts for this by observing that the road hereabouts is passing over rock formations which are impervious to water; deep ditches would be needed to keep the road dry. (Further north, nearer Crosby Ravensworth, the road crosses well-drained limestone, and the ditches are far less evident; Margary, 1957; Ross, 1920).

Standing on the ridge of the road, one looks southwards along the Roman line towards its oblique crossing of the motorway (a line continued, of course, by the remains on the other side of the M6). Looking northwards, beyond the east-west minor road on which Sproat Ghyll stands, field walls continue the straight line of the road as it climbs upwards to the horizon.

North of Sproat Ghyll the course of the Roman road is roughly followed by the track (with right of way) which crosses the east-west road a short distance east of Sproat Ghyll (at 603076). Starting northwards from this road, a mound a little to the east of the track initially marks the line; this gradually merges with the track which is then accompanied by a field wall. The track now veers off to the east, but after a short distance another track, coming from Sproat Ghyll, comes on to the line and follows it northwards to (and beyond) the point where the B6261 is crossed. Along this stretch the Roman line lies west of the field wall; the ridge is prominent in places with remains of the metalling. Higher up the fell, beyond the B6261, large boulders appear along the line (as previously

Figure 18: Looking north along the ridge of the Roman road in the fields south of Sproat Ghyll Farm; the deep ditches are a feature of this stretch. The solitary tree on the horizon stands alongside a field wall (not visible), which continues the line north.

Figure 19: About one mile north of the B6261 looking north; the Roman road runs on the bedrock.

observed south of Sproat Ghyll), and for some distance the road runs on the natural rock surface. Still further on, the line of the road makes a significant change in direction which will be discussed in the next section.

Note on access

Fortunately for the enthusiastic explorer, all the features described in this section can be easily studied. There is no public access to the remains south of the Tebay motorway service area, but with the aid of the Pathfinder map these can be viewed from the southern edge of the area, and the ridge can then be followed northwards through the wood east of the car park.

A short distance north of the M6 a path with right of way comes on to the Roman line and follows it across the rough pasture, a stretch which should by no means be missed.

Section Six

Ewe Close and Wickerslack

(Landranger 91; Pathfinder 597)

North of the crossing of the B6261, the track which we have been following northwards from Sproat Ghyll continues to mark the general line of the Roman road as it commences the ascent of Crosby Ravensworth Fell. But track and road soon leave the western edge of the area covered by Pathfinder 607, and for a short distance are to be found on the eastern edge of O.S. Outdoor Leisure map, no. 7 (English Lakes, South Eastern Area). However not even the most avid enthusiast need contemplate purchasing this extra map, since very soon after, at 599102, on the shoulder of the hill, the Roman road makes a convenient turn from west of north to east of north as indicated at the end of the last section, which brings it back on to the next Pathfinder to the north, No. 597.

This change of direction is at first sight difficult to explain, for there is apparently nothing to prevent the Roman line continuing on its former heading, west of north. This would, in fact, not only keep it high on the ridge which it is presently climbing – a position always favoured by Roman engineers – but would point almost directly to its next destination – the fort at Brougham, just south of Penrith. In fact it could very conveniently reach Brougham by following the route taken by the modern M6 – at this point only 300 or 400 yards to the west. The change of alignment to east of north is actually a definite diversion which not only swings it away from its objective but brings it into more difficult terrain, and for this an explanation is certainly required.

A very probable explanation was offered in 1933 by R.G. Collingwood. He noted that by taking this turn the Roman road pointed directly at the British settlement of Ewe Close, some three miles ahead and the centre of a significant group of settlements in the Crosby Ravensworth area. More will be said about this shortly, at this point we simply note that the presence of these people must have had a real importance for the Romans to bring about such an unexpected diversion in their main western route to the north (Collingwood, 1933).

As it happens, the track we have been following from Sproat Ghyll coincides approximately with the Roman line throughout its change of course, so if we keep to it we shall find ourselves pointing in the right direction, at least for a while. Close attention to the course marked on Pathfinder No. 597 is, however, needed in this area, if we are not to lose the line. A convenient sighting point is Wicker Street Cairn (604117), seen ahead

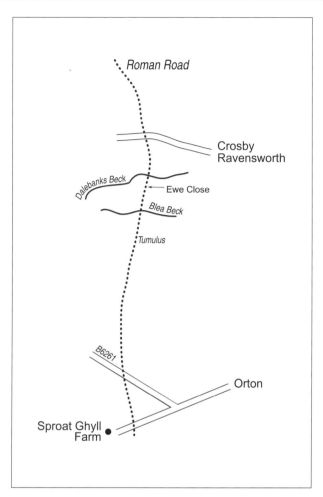

Sketch Map 7: The Roman Road in the area of Crosby Ravensworth (not to scale).

Figure 20: The approach to Blea Beck from the north – a massive ridge between ditches; the faint traces of the road as it climbs the hill opposite are far clearer on the actual site.

on the summit of the hill. (Wicker Street was apparently the traditional name of this section of the road). The cairn marks a tumulus, alongside which a sign proclaims "ancient burial ground"; the Roman road is plainly seen running past the tumulus on its western side, and from this vantage point its line is clear to the north descending to Blea Beck and then climbing the hillside opposite.

Descending towards Blea Beck, which lies about half a mile beyond the tumulus, the raised approach to the beck is very clear indeed. The frequent explorer of these roads will have observed that the ridge on which the Roman engineers normally built their roads often becomes much more marked in the vicinity of a stream or river crossing. Perhaps streams were more liable to overflow in those days – the channels were not kept clear and certainly not canalised as they often are nowadays; hence the surrounding area could become waterlogged and marshy and a well-raised roadway would be a necessity.

In this case the road, as it approaches Blea Beck, has the appearance of a massive ridge between ditches. This is echoed even more strongly on the northern side of the beck. The actual crossing point of the beck (606125), however, appears to be marked by two mounds facing each other skewwise across the stream; these look very much like bridge abutments.

About 500 yards north-east of Blea Beck the open moor ends and the road enters the enclosed fields. Traces continue to be evident right up to the first wall, though not so obvious for the last 100 yards or so. Ewe Close which – as mentioned above – is adjacent to the Roman road, is now not far ahead, but there is no public access from this point. In fact the most convenient approach to the ancient settlement of Ewe Close is from Crosby Ravensworth, along the track (with right of way) which leads south-westwards from the village alongside Dalebanks Beck to Low

Figure 21: The ridge of the Roman road approaching Blea Beck from the south.

Dalebanks Farm. Here permission should be sought to visit Ewe Close. It is clearly marked on the Pathfinder map (No. 597) about a quarter of a mile south of the farm, and is quite easily found, although to the non-specialist the remains of the early settlement appear as simply a series of banks and hollows. But the course of the Roman road, in which we are principally interested, stands out as a bold ridge just to the west of the settlement, of which it virtually forms the western boundary. It continues the same direct north-easterly alignment as at Blea Beck, and the ridge on which it is raised falls away steeply on its western side.

The line intersects the field wall obliquely and then crosses the next field to arrive at Dalebanks Beck at or very near the present ford (610139), by Low Dalebanks Farm, which must surely be the successor of the Roman ford. At the beck crossing, the Roman line changes direction from north-east to almost due north. This is not a point at which such a change would normally be expected; changes of alignment normally occur on high points with a long view ahead rather than down in a valley like this. Evidently the road has completed its diversion and is now resuming its main direction – which seems to confirm that the road altered course to pass close by Ewe Close.

Just north of the Dalebanks Beck the new line of the Roman road passes close to a farm called Harber and a little over half a mile further north it passes two others called High and Low Harberwain. Variants of the name 'harbour' in its Old English sense of 'shelter for wayfarers' are common on Roman roads, and the use of the name here indicates that this stretch probably remained in use after the coming of the Anglian/Norse settlers. 'Harberwain' would presumably mean 'shelter for wagons'.

A path, with right of way, leads north from Harber farm, following a course not far removed from the Roman line and indeed coinciding with

Figure 22: Looking south over the ford across Dalesbank Beck.

29

it for a short distance together with field boundaries. The path ends just short of the east-west Harberwain Lane, but by taking a track which conveniently leads east at this point the course of the Roman road can be clearly seen marked by a double line of trees running south – north across the last field to the south of Harberwain Lane, with a scatter of stones among the trees which might be relics of the metalling. It is rather surprising that this group of trees is not shown on the Pathfinder map; a couple of farm workers confirmed that they are locally recognised as marking the course of the road. North of Harberwain Lane (which is crossed at 609151) the line is continued by a (single) line of trees alongside a wall, and then first by field walls and later by a hollow way northwards to the hamlet of Wickerslack

A track on the line of the road (still following the same alignment – almost due north) connects the farmsteads in Wickerslack and continues northwards between stone walls for a short distance. Two lanes then lead off to east and west, but the course of the Roman road continues heading just west of north, followed by a path with right of way and by field walls. Intermittent signs of the ridge appear, now on one side of the wall, now on the other, replaced at one point by a hollow way.

About half a mile north of Wickerslack the Roman line forms the western boundary of a wood; here the ridge is low but clear. It becomes much more marked as the ford over Low Wood Beck (609116) is approached, immediately south of the south-east corner of Spring Wood. (Pathfinder No. 597 is an indispensable guide throughout all this part of the exploration). At this corner a change of direction more to the north-west occurs, forming a convenient break point in our survey.

Figure 23: Looking north along the line of trees and the wall which mark the course of the Roman road north of Harberwain Lane.

Note on access

As indicated in the text above, the track, with right of way, northwards from Sproat Ghyll continues to follow the Roman line quite closely, even when the latter swings eastwards on its approach to Crosby Ravensworth. However, shortly after this point – at a spot marked on Pathfinder 597 as Coalpit Hill (602111) – the footpath swings away to the north-west while the Roman road continues on its alignment a few degrees east of north. Beyond this point it is not marked as a right of way, but is very evident as a track across the open moor, and as indicated above, Wicker Street Cairn , which lies just to the east of the Roman line a short distance north of Coalpit Hill, is a good indication of the direction it takes. From the Cairn the course is clear down to Blea Beck and then up the opposite side of the valley to the beginning of the enclosed land.

Directions for reaching Ewe Close are in the body of the section. Northwards from Harber Farm a footpath with right of way runs close to the Roman line, coinciding with it (and the field walls which follow it) for some distance. The track continues north of Harberwain Lane (though without right of way) to Wickerslack, and runs a field's width west of the line of walls which continue to follow the Roman line. At Wickerslack a track, once again with right of way, takes up the course of the Roman road and continues it northwards to the crossing of Low Wood Beck and beyond. The reader will have noticed that throughout this area footpaths and/or field boundaries mark the road almost continuously.

Section Seven

The approach to Brougham

(Landranger 91 & 90 ; Pathfinder 597 & Outdoor Leisure Map 5)

The change of direction noted at the end of the last section, which brought the road on to a new alignment more to the north-west, occurs immediately after the crossing of Low Wood Beck. Both Ross and Margary agree that the course of the road on this new alignment is first followed for about 300 yards by the straight metalled track which forms the eastern boundary of Spring Wood (and which is very visible before Low Wood Beck is reached, thus giving a clear view, on the ground, of this change of alignment). (Ross, 1920; Margary, 1957). Actually a ridge appears to enter the wood at its southern end, just west of the track, with which it merges a little further on. The track itself runs as a terrace for some distance with distinct signs of engineering. It turns away eastwards at the northern edge of Spring Wood, but the Roman line continues on the same north-western alignment. After leaving Spring Wood the line of the road is followed, though only approximately, by the western boundary of Reagill Grange plantation and then by the stretch of road on the west of Reagill village. North of the village it appears that the present road lies west of the Roman line as Sleagill is approached, but shortly before reaching the village it swings east across the line, crossing the bridge over Sleagill Beck. Just west of this bridge is the ford (607192) which marks the probable crossing point of the Roman road.

The road from Sleagill to Newby Head now takes up the line and follows it with general directness, as the Pathfinder map shows (actually the North Eastern Lakes Leisure area map, which replaces the Pathfinder for this section. Since, however, the area in question is small, the explorer might manage for the moment with the one-inch Landranger). The straightness of the road is not quite so evident on the ground; local variations make it appear quite winding. It is noticeable that nearly all the roads which follow the general course of this particular Roman road are nowadays very minor – even though, in its day, it was a most important through route, it manages to keep clear of almost all of the routes chosen by its principal modern successors.

Almost exactly one mile north of Sleagill the present road crosses (591205) another beck by a bridge, immediately west of which are distinct signs of a ford, with a cutting slanting down the north bank. The modern road then veers off eastwards for a while to reach Newby Head; the course of the Roman road continues through the field west of the

Figure 24: Looking south-east along the track which follows the line of the Roman road along the eastern edge of Spring Wood; terraced and level.

village, and then passes under (or very near) the old (and interesting) Quaker cemetery south-east of Lamsmere. Most enthusiasts will be willing to forget their Roman preoccupations for a few moments to explore this fascinating burial place.

South of Syke House there are signs of the Roman ridge in the fields to the west converging on the present road, which rejoins the Roman line soon after. It then follows the Roman alignment rigidly for over a mile, passing en route, on its eastern side, the significantly named Street Head Wood, and further along, Street House, also alongside the road on its eastern edge. Indeed Ross reports that the whole of this straight stretch was formerly called 'The Street', a very strong indication of Roman origin.

A quarter of a mile beyond Street House the present road turns sharply to the north-east at the south edge of a wood. A faint ridge, pointed out by Margary and just discernible, continues the Roman line into this wood – it causes a very slight hump in the path which crosses it just before the wood is entered. Ross and Margary agree that the course of the Roman road is continued for a quarter of a mile on the same alignment by a fence which passes Gilshaughlin House (Ross, 1920; Margary, 1957). At the (northern) end of this fence a new alignment is commenced in a direction rather more west of north, pointing to the fort at Brougham, the next fort on this route.

This would carry the road across open country, and, rather surprisingly, no traces have been found for the next two miles or so; certainly neither paths nor field boundaries seem to indicate its course. But at Moorhouses, about half a mile short of the fort, a straight length of minor road comes on to the line and continues it for the remaining distance to the fort. In fact the site of the fort itself lies in the angle of this road (or its continuation, Mill Lane) and the B6262 as Penrith is approached. In the field just west of Mill Lane and north of the B6262 a bank and ditch mark

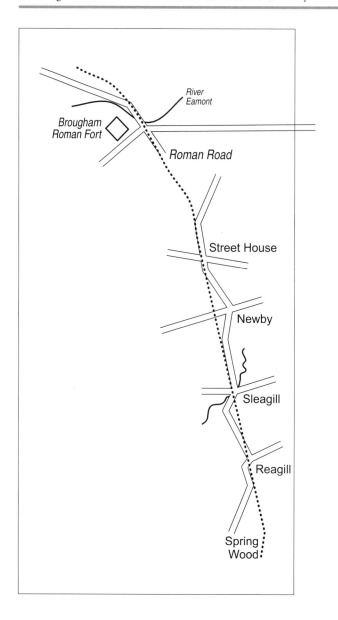

Sketch Map 8: The Roman Road in the southern approach to Brougham Fort (not to scale).

the outline of the fort, and some of the tombstones uncovered during excavation are preserved in the buildings of the adjoining Norman Castle, together with other monumental Roman inscriptions.

Especially important is a milestone, found in the area and currently located in the Castle ticket office, which carries an inscription concluding with the letters 'R P C CAR'. It has been established that this is an abbreviation of 'Respublica Civitatis Carvetiorum' i.e. the Commonwealth of the tribe of the Carvetii. This is conclusive evidence for the existence of the Carvetii (referred to previously on page 11 of this volume) a people

Figure 25: The ford across Sleagill Beck marking the probable crossing point of the Roman road; it lies just west of the bridge on the present Reagill/Sleagill road and just south of the Sleagill crossroads.

who, before and during the Roman epoch, occupied much or all of modern Cumbria. (Higham and Jones, 1985).

At the fort of Brougham the road which we have been following is joined from the east by that other magnificent trans-Pennine Roman road which has now become the modern A66 for practically the whole of its length. In fact these last few yards are an exception; the A66 swings north of the Roman line a quarter of a mile away, leaving the junction to be effected by the minor road which completes the distance.

Note on access

From Spring Wood north to Newby and onwards to Street House the present road is never far from the Roman line, and there are plenty of side roads and paths to give access to the latter. But from Gilshaughlin to Brougham both access and traces are, for the most part, missing. The general alignment, however, is followed for the last half mile or so by the by-road to Moorhouses, and the interested explorer might look for traces along this line south-eastwards towards Gilshaughlin.

Ross, whose opinion is always worth heeding, considers that the road between Gilshaughlin Wood and Moorhouses may not have been completely straight but may have bent somewhat to avoid the swampy ground around the River Leith; this would render its exact course difficult to ascertain; it seems just possible that the straight length of road which arrives at Moorhouses from the south-west might be a linking alignment (Ross 1930).

Section Eight

Brougham to Carlisle

(Landranger 90, 86, 85; Pathfinder 557, 568, 558)

This section describes one of those awkward stretches which, ideally, involve several O.S. maps, as detailed above, but since practically the whole route is covered by modern roads – and main roads at that – there is not the same need for large-scale maps at this point, and the reader might well feel able to dispense with them. In parentheses, we might note that, apart from the urban areas just north of Manchester, this is virtually the only stretch of the long Roman road from Manchester to Carlisle which has been overlaid by modern road-builders – by no means the least of the attractions of this great historic thoroughfare.

The road passed the fort at Brougham on its eastern side, joined here, as noted above, by another important early Roman road, coming by way of Stainmore from what is now Scotch Corner. Margary notes (volume 2, page 228) that this link road joins the Brougham/Carlisle road (which he calls the 'trunk road') in the middle of its alignment, thus indicating that the trunk road is the earlier of the two (Margary, 1957). After crossing the river Eamont the Brougham/Carlisle road continued north-westwards through the eastern suburbs of what is now the town of Penrith. Not until the built-up area is passed do further traces occur in the form of the eastern boundaries of three successive fields immediately north of the minor road which goes north-eastwards to North Dykes. This line of fences leads to a point (508324) almost half a mile north of Bleak House on the minor road running north from Penrith to the east of the A6 (which it leaves at its southern end and rejoins at its northern end). The Roman line then swings to the north and is followed by this minor road, which shows the typical appearance of a modern by-road following the course of a Roman road (straight, raised, wide verges – see picture on page 38).

Shortly after passing Greengill Foot the roundabout is reached at which this road rejoins the A6; the Roman line passes just east of the roundabout and then coincides with the A6, which now follows the course, with local variations, almost all the way to Carlisle. This obviously results in the obliteration of all traces apart from the rigid alignment, but the journey north is not without interest. Some four miles north of the roundabout the site of the fort of Voreda (Old Penrith) is passed, immediately west of the road (at 493385), with a farmstead adjoining. The raised, rectangular, level fort platform, with its eastern edge parallel to the road, the site of the east gate, and the north-east rampart corner are all very clear.

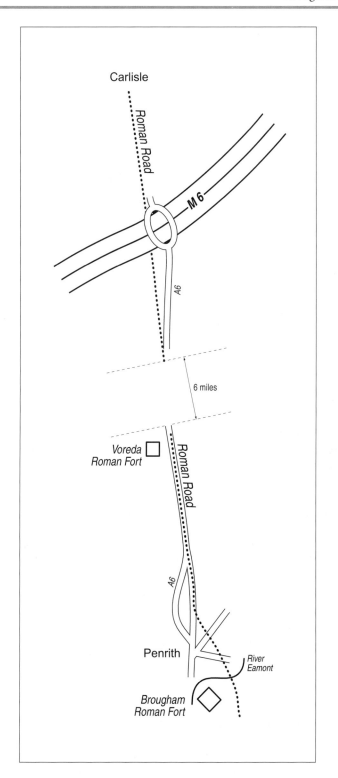

Sketch Map 9: The Road between Penrith and Carlisle (not to scale).

Figure 26: The road described above, viewed from north of Greengill Foot, looking south.

Stones in some of the field walls and farm buildings adjoining bear hatch-markings indicating that they may have come from the fort (Austen, 1991).

About five miles north of Plumpton the A6 veers west to by-pass High Hesket; the course of the Roman road runs straight on through the village – it appears well raised but all other features are obscured by the buildings. Afterwards the A6 rejoins the Roman line and remains with it for another four miles, until just before reaching Scalesceugh Hall. Here the A6 swerves to the east, and then runs for three miles on a roughly parallel course a short distance away from the Roman line. The latter continues ahead on a course, marked for much of the way by field boundaries, which brings it quite close to the river Petteril. Its line can be investigated (though there is not a great deal to see) by following a track which leads westwards from the A6 about half a mile south of its intersection with the M6 – not far north of Springfield Farm. The course of the Roman road crosses this track at a point (441510) where the latter bends southwards, with a side track going off to the north-west; a hedge-line running south-east/north-west marks the marks the line, accurately to the north, less so southwards, where the Roman line slants away westwards. The view to the north along the hedge is blocked by trees, but in fact it follows the alignment across several fields, as far as the road junction mentioned above – junction no. 42 on the motorway. North of the junction the course of the Roman road is rendered uncertain by the encroachments on to the line of the river Petteril, which may perhaps have changed its course since Roman times. There seems no doubt, however, that north of Carlton the A6 rejoins the Roman line and stays with it for the remaining distance to Carlisle (the Roman *Luguvalium*).

In Carlisle itself the line of the A6, and of its Roman predecessor, is taken up by Botchergate, leading towards the northern part of the town where was situated the early fort. For an archaeological survey of Roman

Figure 27: The north rampart and ditch of the Roman fort of Voreda, viewed from the A6, which here follows the Roman line.

Carlisle, and an account of its history, development and importance, the reader is referred to the excellent essay by Dr. David Shotter at the end of this volume. Here one should perhaps add that the only remains of fort and civilian settlement now visible are in the garden of the Tullie House Museum, which houses a notable collection of Roman artefacts which the enthusiast will certainly wish to see.

Note on access

Apart from the exceptions noted in the text, this portion of the route is followed by modern (main) roads, which of course poses its own problems for the enthusiast, since the only practical way to follow the route is to drive along it. However, there are parking places and sidewalks which make it possible, for example, to have a good look at the fort of Voreda, adjacent to the road. The short length from which the A6 diverts, south of the motorway junction (no. 42), may be explored by taking the pathway indicated above in the body of the section, though, as indicated there, there is little to see bar fences and hedges marking the line.

Part Two: Branch Roads

Section Nine

Branch Road No. 1. The road from Burrow-in-Lonsdale to Lancaster.

(Landranger 97; Pathfinder 637, 628)

(Since most of the route postulated for this road follows present-day roads, it is not thought necessary to illustrate this section with a sketch map; the Landranger and Pathfinder maps will supply all the guidance needed).

The road north-eastwards (along the Lune) from Lancaster to Burrow-in-Lonsdale (to reverse the direction set out in the section heading) is a particularly interesting one, since it may well represent a very early Roman line of approach from the south to Lonsdale and onwards to Carlisle. There is an increasing amount of evidence to indicate that amphibious operations were important in the initial phase of the conquest of the north west, with sea-borne troops and supplies disembarking in the estuaries and advancing by way of the river valleys, perhaps in concert with others moving overland. The Lune valley would be of very great strategic importance in this context. Thus the two lines of advance represented later by the Ribchester/Burrow and the Lancaster/Burrow roads may have been contemporary, or perhaps the latter was the earlier of the two (Shotter, 1992; Shotter & White, 1995).

The foregoing considerations make it attractive to survey this route north-eastwards, starting at the Lancaster end. The road to be followed ran south of the Lune; there may have been a road along the north bank also (Leather, 1972), but if so it has left far fewer traces. Margary (and Codrington before him) would see the road, south of the Lune, branching from the main coastal northern route (Margary 70) at Scotforth, about a mile and a half south of the fort of Lancaster. For most of its length to Burrow the Roman route, again according to Margary, would be mainly represented by roads still in use. If Margary's postulated route is accepted – and he devotes only 14 lines to describing the road – it must be conceded that the road in detail is far from straight, though the general line between its south-western end and its north-eastern end at Burrow -in-Lonsdale is remarkably direct, and quite often it traverses difficult stretches in short alignments, typically Roman, rather than on a truly winding course (Codrington, 1918; Margary, 1957).

Still following Margary, the first mile or so from the junction at Scotforth is uncertain, but then the very straight length of Newlands Road comes on to the line for just over a mile, terraced along the hillside and, as Margary points out, commanding wide views across the Lune to the west. At the north-eastern end of Newlands Road the Roman road would seem to bear to the right (eastwards) – still followed by a modern road – to avoid climbing a steep hill, and then, after a short distance, resume its former north-eastern direction for almost a mile. Towards the end of this stretch the road enters Knott's Wood and becomes a terraceway along the steep hillside, with a steep climb to the left (west) and a steep drop on the right (east).

After traversing this quite difficult section, the present road (Quernmore Road), at Posterngate, bends to the right (eastwards) through an angle of about 60 degrees, but there seems no reason why the Roman road should not have continued straight ahead, following a direction almost aligned with Newlands Road behind and also with the short stretch of the present road when it comes back on to this line (at 525631) in approaching Deys Farm, a mile ahead. (A glance at Pathfinder 637 will clarify this and succeeding sentences). On reaching the beginning of this short stretch to Deys Farm, the explorer will find that its direction is continued backwards (southwestwards) by an old track, which after a few yards runs along a definite ridge, with ditches on each side, lined with oak trees. However, after a short distance south-westwards this track is interrupted by Shellhouse pond, which may be a relatively recent construction (the ground is part of Quernmore Park); failing that, if this really is the Roman line, a diversion will have been necessary.

Returning to the present road, as it approaches Deys Farm, the general direction north-east is continued as a curving terraceway along the hillside, avoiding low ground to the west. Shortly afterwards the modern road turns very sharply to the south, and a track continues the north-eastern direction, crossing the deep gorge of Artle Beck by a bridge. It was in the

Figure 28: Looking north-east along the track described in the text.

bed of this beck that an inscribed Hadrianic milestone (now in the Lancaster Museum) was found in 1803 after a storm flood (Leather, 1972). The find spot was about half a mile downstream from the bridge just mentioned, but it is evident that Artle Beck is a torrent in flood conditions – (it was reported to have risen 12 feet after the storm of 1803) – and the milestone could easily have travelled this distance over the centuries. Consequently it is reasonable to accept the modern bridge, which is on the general line between Scotforth and Burrow-in-Lonsdale, as being at or near the Roman crossing point.

Beyond the beck a track, with right of way, slants uphill to the north and then resumes the north-easterly line to the outskirts of Caton, arriving in St. Anne's Close, off Littledale Road. The track is embanked on its north side for most of its length and runs as a terraceway along the hillside to the north, keeping a good level. The line is interrupted by Caton village but resumed about a quarter of a mile beyond, running as a direct minor road through Caton Green and past Hole House to fall into the main A683 road at the brickworks south-west of Claughton.

Margary suggests that the A683 represents the Roman line onwards from this point through Hornby, Melling and Tunstall to Burrow-in-Lonsdale. It certainly continues the general direction and runs, as Margary indicates, in straight lengths; this is possibly more evident on the smaller scale Landranger map (Margary, 1957). Moreover it closely follows the course of the Lune, keeping to the edge of the higher ground south of the river. The short straight length pointing slightly north of west through Hornby may be regarded as a linking alignment, the road resuming its north-eastern course along the edge of the valley afterwards.

Where the modern road swings to the east north of Melling to cross the Greta at Greta Bridge, the previous line is continued northwards by a strong line of four field walls, lining up with the straight stretch north

Figure 29: Fragment of Roman carved stone built into the west wall of a barn on the east side of the A683 just north of the entrance to Burrow Hall.

of Tunstall beyond the river; this suggests that the Roman crossing may have been downstream from the present one. The very straight stretch north of Tunstall just mentioned is very striking, aiming directly for the fort at Burrow-in-Lonsdale.

The site of the fort lies within the grounds of Burrow Hall, beyond Leck Beck, and the modern road swings west to pass it. Just beyond the main gate, alongside the entrance to Yew Tree Farm on the eastern side of the road, part of a carved stone from the fort cemetery is built into the west wall of a roadside barn. The explorer is warned, however, that fast traffic makes this a dangerous place to stop and look.

Note on access
The only substantial part of this route not followed by a modern road – the path from Artle Mill to Caton – is followed by a track with right of way.

Section Ten

Branch Road No 2. From Burrow-in-Lonsdale to the North-West

(Landranger 97; Pathfinder 628, 637, 627)

Only the first part – ten miles or so – of this road is known, and even over this section the course is only intermittently evident. It is nevertheless a striking road; it merits ten lines in Margary, (under the title "Whittington to Lupton") and it was the subject of an interesting survey by Dr. Francis Villy in 1936. Its starting point is not in doubt – directly from the fort at Burrow-in-Lonsdale or branching from some road near it – and from its general direction its destination would seem to be Watercrook, near Kendal (Margary, 1957; Villy, 1937).

A promising point to start the investigation is at 610763, on the west bank of the Lune directly east of Whittington and about half a mile northwest of the fort. Here a track, with right of way, heads due west from the river, which at this point looks quite fordable. Viewed from the opposite (east) bank, there are distinct signs of a terrace sloping up the west bank of the river in an upstream direction to access the end of the track. Rivers, of course, frequently change direction over a period approaching 2000 years, so too much importance must not be attached to these features. It is however worth mentioning that another track on the eastern side of the Lune, also running east-west, reaches the river a few yards downstream from our starting point.

For the first 200 yards the track (west of the river) is quite straight and heavily metalled; it crosses a stream by a footbridge and then curves up a slope through a shallow cutting. As it approaches the (modern) road near Cockin House it is quite steeply banked, indicating that this stretch, at least, may be on the Roman line, since its direction fits in with the known course further on.

If the modern road is followed westwards from Cockin House, it skirts the northern edge of Whittingon and continues westwards past High House on the right (north); it then bends sharply northwards, then to the north-east and finally to north of east, straightening out for about 200 yards. This straight stretch is the first certain piece of Roman road; at its end, when the present road swings northwards again (at 591768), a straight line of four field walls continues the line directly ahead, with traces of the ridge on each side. In just over half a mile the present road comes back on the line (at 582770) and follows it for about 100 yards to near Nanny

45

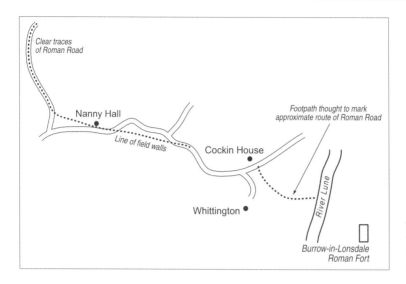

Sketch Map 10: The Southern Section of Branch Road No. 2 (not to scale).

Hall (all this is very plainly seen on the Pathfinder maps 628 and 637). Here the present road veers to the south and once again a field wall takes up the line, which is then lost in an area of extensive quarrying. At Battle House the present road to Hutton Roof comes on or near the line, following it closely as it swings north to avoid Hutton Roof Crags.

After passing Hutton Roof Crags, the Roman line is taken up by the minor road that forks left (at 568791) to Newbiggin about two-fifths of a mile north of Hutton Roof. As this road approaches Newbiggin it bends to the west for a short distance and then resumes its former line, which it holds for the remainder of this survey. Just north-west of Newbiggin Farm, the Roman ridge appears strongly in the field south-west of the

Figure 30: The embanked track (at 603763) approaching the (modern) road near Cockin House from the south.

46

present road (see picture) indicating that the latter is only an approximate guide along this stretch.

Immediately north of this, at Town End Farm, commences the most spectacular section of the road. To quote from Villy "The (present) road changes its character from a minor country lane of slightly winding course to an imposing structure laid out in straight lengths" – in other words it now rigidly follows the Roman line instead of only giving its general direction. And the Roman engineers laid out the next mile or so with skill that is evident even now. To quote Villy once more, "A well banked-up terrace some eighteen feet wide runs along the hillside (the flank of Farleton Fell, sloping steeply down from the left, or west) and carries the present way of only about nine feet on its crown". Villy implies that the Roman road would probably have been considerably wider, and this, of course, is highly probable. For the first part of this section the terraceway is somewhat masked by hedges and walls, but further north the road runs free of these and its configuration is more apparent (Villy, 1937).

For those who explore them on foot, these Roman roads often have other attractions unconnected with archaeology, especially in their remoter reaches. When I last visited this particular section, in company with a friend, we were much distracted by the sight of a group of buzzards circling above Farleton Fell. I cannot recall ever seeing so many together.

It is something of an anticlimax to add that at the end of this stretch, when the northern end of Farleton Fell is reached, the road regains its insignificant character and veers westwards away from the Roman line. Furthermore, nothing so far seems to have been recorded of any further traces. If the road was heading for Kendal as its immediate objective, its course might well have been obscured by canal construction, but it would be very surprising if recognisable lengths have not survived.

Figure 31: The ridge of the road crossing a field (at 556795) near Newbiggin Farm.

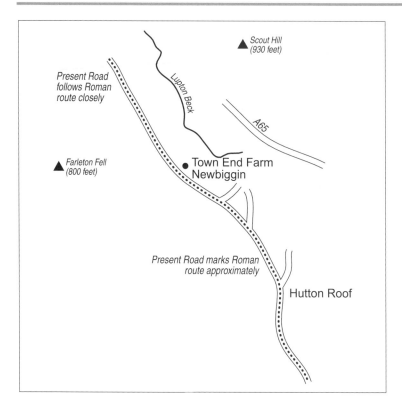

Sketch Map 11: The Northern Section of Branch Road No. 2 (not to scale).

Figure 32: Looking north-west along the road, about $^{1}/_{4}$ mile north-west of Town End Farm; the road is running along a broad terrace on the hillside.

48

Figure 33: Looking north-west along the Roman road (or its successor) about ³/₄ mile north-west of Town End Farm. The road is very straight and runs along a broad terrace often masked by hedges.

Note on access

The track from the Lune to Cockin House, referred to in the text, is right of way throughout. Most of the course followed west of Whittington is along or near present roads. The gap west of Cockin House might repay investigation, also the stretch west of Nanny Hall, though quarrying has probably destroyed most traces here.

Section Eleven

Branch Road No. 3 Low Borrow Bridge to the South-West (Watercrook?)

(Landranger 91, 97; Pathfinder 607, Outdoor Leisure 7
[English Lakes S.E.])

Just north of the fort of Low Borrow Bridge a side road led off in the direction of Watercrook, near Kendal, some ten miles distant. It is clearly traceable only for the first few miles, where it traverses rough country and leaves very interesting traces. Though briefly described by Margary, it does not seem to have been extensively studied, and the only survey I have come across was recorded over a century ago by T. Wilson (Margary, 1957; Wilson, 1883).

Its starting point is indicated by the road which forks west from the Carlingill road just beyond the fort, and runs under the railway, the M6, and the A685, and thence along the south side of Borrow Beck to become an access road, or track (macadamised) to the farms higher up the dale. About a mile from the fort it crosses a small stream (at 599015); nowadays this is bridged but in former times there was evidently a ford adjacent. The track now continues to follow the beck, leaving the Roman road, which turns south-west to climb out of the valley.

For a short distance the Roman road follows the west bank of a tributary stream before turning further to the south and beginning the ascent. In this area it is of robust construction, being impressively hewn out of the rock for a short distance. Further on it enters boggy ground and for a while is difficult to trace. Then it goes through a gate in a long field wall (at 595012) and joins a footpath (with right of way) which has left the valley floor some distance to the west of the bridge mentioned above; (after the junction the right of way conveniently accompanies the Roman road over the hill). The road now seems to follow the wall directly up the hillside northwards for about 200 yards. An alternative route is provided here by an elaborate series of zigzag which seems of recent date, not being mentioned in Wilson's account or figuring on the first edition of the one-inch O.S. map (David & Charles reprint, Newton Abbot, 1979).

The robust construction noted as the Roman route leaves the valley floor is evident throughout its course up the north side of the Whinfell ridge, with several stretches in which the rock has been cut away to allow or ease the passage of the road. Further up the hill the road appears as a hard green track, easy to follow, with occasional signs of metalling and with the ditches frequently marked by growth of reeds or coarse grass.

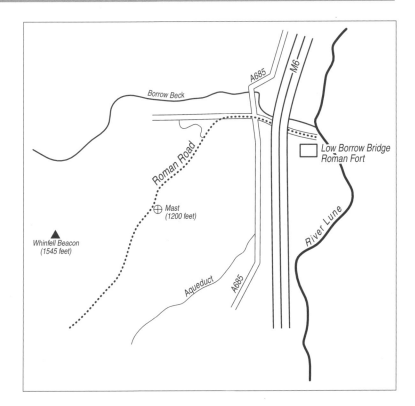

Sketch Map 12: The Roman Road leading south-west from Low Borrow Bridge (not to scale).

Figure 34: Looking south-west along the Roman road at point 597014, shortly after it has left the track alongside Borrow Beck to climb the hillside; the road is impressively hewn out of the rock.

Towards the summit it is sometimes impressively terraced along the hill-side; It is generally about 12 feet wide. On the summit of the ridge it passes just west of the mast marked as 'Repeater Station' on the O.S. maps. From this point an extensive view southward opens up, with Kendal clearly visible in the distance.

The track continues to follow the course of the Roman road as it descends the north side of the ridge; it is described as a hard green road-way by both Wilson and Margary, but nowadays it has been concreted over north of the summit, presumably in connexion with the building and maintenance of the repeater station. Consequently its course as a whole is more visible – an elongated zigzag to suit the slope, though the map still shows it to be very direct. Drainage culverts, now modernised, cross it; the first of these, about 200 yards south of the repeater station, still gives a glimpse of its original rough construction.

The course of the road on to Watercrook is, in detail at least, rather uncertain, and a sketch map at this point would probably not be helpful. Both Wilson and Margary suggest that Cockin Farm (at the foot of the hill) and The Borrans, a mile further on (the name may be significant) are on the line. Viewed from the summit, the course of the road certainly seems to point in this direction, but about 700 yards before reaching Cockin the present track veers southward, though it is taken up again by a lane at the farm. From the Borrans, minor roads carry the line on to Patton Bridge, Meal Bank and so to Kendal and Watercrook. There is a brief stretch of straight road not far south of Patton Bridge which is continued for a mile by a rigidly straight stretch of field walls not far off the line, but in this region of straight walls this may not be significant. Otherwise indications hitherto have been lacking, though they may of course await discovery.

However the traces left by this road on the Whinfell ridge – especially on its north face – are so interesting, and apparently so little recorded, that, rather than offering conjectures on its subsequent course, it is thought preferable to complete this section with a few extra illustrations of these earlier traces.

Figure 35: Looking south along the road where it is followed by the old wall; the rock has been cut away on the right (west) side; the wall runs along the left (east) side.

Figure 36: Still on the lower slopes of the north face, looking north-eastwards towards Borrowdale; the ditches are well marked by the growth of coarse grass, and there are traces of metalling on the central ridge.

Figure 37: Higher up the north face, and looking southwards towards the summit, the road appears to run through a shallow cutting, and the vegetation on the left (east) bank evidently conceals a rock cutting like those which remain exposed along the road further down.

Figure 38: About 250 yards from the summit, the road appears as a hard green track terraced along the hillside.

Figure 39: The final approach, from the north, to the summit of the Whinfell ridge; the road points directly to the repeater station on the crest.

Figure 40: The (macadamised) road zigzagging down the southern face of the Whinfell ridge; the mast of the repeater station is seen on the horizon.

Note on access

The only portion of the route over Whinfell described above which is not either public road or right of way is the short length of track between 599015 (bridge over stream) and 595012 (gate in long wall). Most of the conjectured route south-west of Whinfell is likewise accessible.

Appendix: The Roman Road from Manchester to Ribchester

1. The Fort of *Mancunium*

(Landranger 109; Pathfinder 724, 713)

The Roman Fort of *Mancunium* (to use the traditionally received version of the Latin form) gave its name to modern Manchester, but little else originally associated with it survives visibly nowadays. The site is well known, west of the south end of Deansgate, in one of the busiest areas of the city; and in fact until the end of the eighteenth century the ramparts and ditches, at any rate, were clearly visible. The district was known as Castlefield because of the Roman fort, which occupied five acres (with an additional civil settlement) alongside the River Medlock, not far east of its junction with the Irwell. The construction across the site, first of the Rochdale canal, then of the railway, effectively obliterated all traces of the fort, with the exception of a mass of masonry within one of the arches of the viaduct leading to Central Station.

However, limited excavations have been possible, notably in 1906/7 by F.A. Bruton, 1965/7 by J.H. Williams and J. Webster, and 1972 by G.D.B. Jones (Jones, 1974), and much has been learned both about the fort itself and the civilian settlement which accompanied it. Moreover, in recent years the Castlefield area has declined in importance as a centre of industry and communications, and in fact it has now been declared a conservation area and has become Britain's first Urban Heritage Park. Among other features there have been reconstructions of various parts of the Roman fort, including the north gate, so that the visitor can contemplate a replica, at least (and read the quite fascinating account of the details of the reconstruction of the gate). A Visitors' Information Centre and a couple of museums add to the attractions of the site.

The fort of *Mancunium,* rectangular in shape like so many Roman forts, was not aligned on the cardinal points of the compass; the 'north' wall and gate faced roughly 30 degrees east of north, and the road which issued from the gate set off in that direction. Like most forts, *Mancunium* went through various phases of development in its history, from its foundation – probably in AD 79 – until its abandonment at the end of the Roman period in the fourth century.

In the photograph (on page 56), the road shown issuing from the north gate (a modern reconstruction, like the gate and ramparts) is on the line of the original Roman road, which apparently remained in use throughout the lifetime of the fort and was shown by the excavators to have been resurfaced at least ten times.

Though it is tempting to think of this road as the first stage of our journey from Manchester to Carlisle, it was in fact what might be called

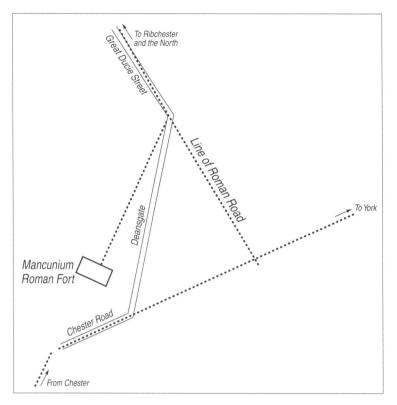

Sketch Map 13: The Roman Road System in the vicinity of the Fort at Manchester (not to scale).

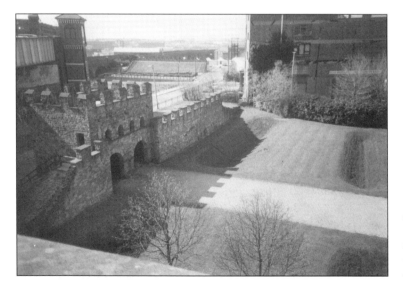

Figure 41: The reconstructed north gate of Mancunium from the outside, showing defensive ditches.

Figure 42: Manchester Roman Fort; the reconstructed west rampart from the outside, showing its defensive ditches.

a neighbourhood road, linking *Mancunium* with the main road heading north, which was joined near the present Cathedral.

In fact, as the sketch map on page 56 shows, the main road north to Carlisle and the Wall began a short distance east of the fort, branching off from the Chester/York road in a manner which suggests that the latter was the earlier road. As the sketch map also shows, the main road north by-passed the fort of *Mancunium,* in very much the same manner as, further north it by-passed the fort of Ribchester, and indeed the fort at Burrow-in-Lonsdale, the next two forts on the journey north. To all three forts the road is joined by neighbourhood roads.

Figure 43: Inside the fort, with the reconstructed footings of a granary in the foreground, and the interior of the reconstructed western defences in the background.

In the immediate vicinity of the site of *Mancunium* the Roman roads have not determined the layout and direction of present-day roads, but elsewhere in the city considerable portions of Roman roads are reflected in the modern street network, as will become more evident later in this study.

Note on access.
There is free access to the site of Mancunium, with its reconstructed gate and defences, and the reader will gather from the text above that these are well worth exploring.

The two museums mentioned at the beginning of the section are of general – not Roman – interest, but there is a Visitors' Information Centre (330 Deansgate) which is open Monday to Saturday.

2. Through the suburbs and along Watling Street

(Landranger 109; Pathfinder 713, 712, 700)

As indicated in the last section, the road which left the north gate of the fort of *Mancunium* in a north-easterly direction joined the main Roman road to the north, heading north-west, in the vicinity of the modern Cathedral, and shortly afterwards the line of this main road is taken up by-roads which still remain in use, first by Great Ducie Street and then by the Bury New Road, which continues the Roman north-western alignment for some considerable distance through the urban areas of Broughton and Prestwich.

From its name Bury New Road is obviously a turnpike road, and is an indication that the Roman route must still have been recognisable – if not, indeed a thoroughfare still in use – when turnpike roads were being laid out at the beginning of the nineteenth century. Nowadays it is the only indication of the Roman line in this area. One notes from the map that Bury New Road swerves a little eastwards in Higher Broughton, a divergence which may well be original, avoiding the floodplain of the Irwell. Bends to the north of this are not so readily accounted for, but the road is certainly back on the Roman alignment as it passes through Prestwich, finally leaving the line as the M62 is approached.

For some distance ahead, north of the M62 crossing, building and road developments have obscured the traces, which, however, seem to have been both plentiful and evident until quite recently. Earlier accounts (Just, 1842 and Watkin, 1883) describe various features which marked the line hereabouts, such as remains of the *agger*, scatters of gravel, lines of fence or hedgerow. The first one-inch map of the area to be published by the O.S. (O.S. 1843; David & Charles reprint 1979) indicates the line quite clearly at frequent intervals as "Roman Road"- as indeed it does throughout the length of the route from Manchester to Ribchester. Even nowadays traces of the Roman line must still be discernible; some will be pointed out below, others await rediscovery by local enthusiasts.

Immediately north of the M62 crossing, there is a gap of about a mile, and then the A665 (Higher Lane) comes on to the line for a short distance. The valley of the river Roch now intervenes, in crossing which local variations in the alignment may have been necessary. North of Radcliffe footpaths (with right of way) east of Crow Trees Farm and beyond from Doffer Fold to Higher Spen Moor Farm run near the line; these tracks may have been diverted by the construction of Withins Reservoir; there are signs of a ridge in places but in general they are rather featureless.

North of the A58 the line is marked by the east boundary of the triangular wedge of fields on the east side of road B6292 to Starling (the Pathfinder maps listed at the head of the section are essential throughout this section). This length, passing along the rear of the houses on the edge of a modern estate, seems nowadays not accessible to the public – a pity, since Margary describes the ridge as especially prominent hereabouts

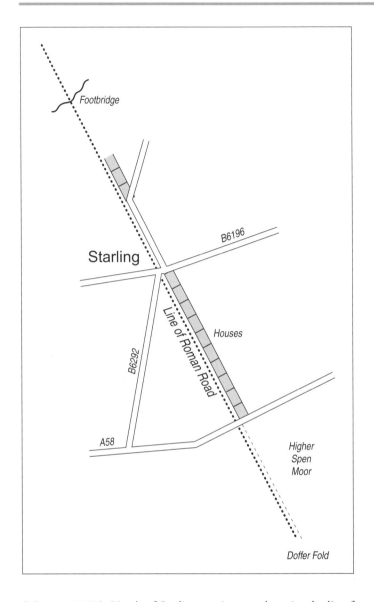

Sketch Map 14: The Roman Road in the vicinity of Starling (not to scale).

(Margary, 1957). North of Starling a minor road carries the line forwards for 200 or 300 yards; this then turns sharply eastwards and the line is continued by a sunken lane, which descends steeply to a stream, now crossed transversely by a footbridge.

North of the stream the lane veers away to the east, but the Roman line continues its north-westerly course, skirting the reservoir on the west. For over a mile beyond this the road is marked neither by tracks nor by field boundaries, but at an intermediate stage, in the fields east of Height Barn, there seem to be traces of a ridge on or near the line. This is especially evident when viewed in profile from a point (764122) north of Height Barn on the road leading south-west from Four Lane Ends.

About 600 yards further north-west, near Isherwood's farm, the line is taken up for over one-and-a-half miles by the impressively straight length of minor road known traditionally as Watling Street and still so named on signboards. Watling Street is the name given to several stretches of Roman road in various parts of the country – not, of course, by the Romans, but by our early English forbears. According to Ekwall, the name is ultimately derived from *Waetlingaceaster,* an ancient (Old English) name of St. Alban's, the Roman *Verulamium* (Ekwall, 1971). The name Watling Street would first be applied to the Roman road from London to St. Alban's, and afterwards, by transfer, to other stretches of Roman road. Since the road from London to St. Alban's was in fact the great Roman highway to the north-west, it could be argued that this Lancashire stretch is a continuation, but by the time it was given its name the road would probably have degenerated into discontinuous stretches.

This section of undoubted Roman road is unusual insofar as it passes through the village of Affetside. Roman roads, essentially means of rapid communication, tended to ignore such amenities as springs or other water sources needed by later settlers, so that they are usually remarkably free of medieval villages. That this village is certainly ancient is shown by the presence of the old cross, which stands on the west side of the road about 200 yards north of the Packhorse Inn – another sign that this road and village were used by travellers before modern forms of transport were thought of. The 'cross' itself, though it stands on a three tier circular stone base in the manner of village crosses, nowadays takes the form of a circular gritstone pillar. It is at least highly probable that this replaces the 'Pilgrim Cross' referred to hereabouts in ancient charters; indeed, it is still known locally as Affetside Cross and is so marked on the O.S. maps.

Ancient crosses are another feature of Roman roads which merit a word

Figure 44: Affetside Cross, looking north-west along Watling Street.

or two. There is at least one other on the road we are following, and several others mark Roman roads in other parts of Lancashire. Some of them may have originated as indicators of the parish boundaries which so often follow Roman lines – indeed the first edition of the one-inch O.S. map for this district, based on a survey made in the mid-1840s, shows a parish boundary following this stretch of Watling street. Codrington, writing some 60 years later, also makes reference to this, though I cannot find any such boundary on the present O.S. map (David and Charles, 1970; Codrington, 1918).

Note on access
A good deal of this first major section of the road (i.e. up to Ribchester) is followed by later thoroughfares; some of these lack interest, for example Bury New Road, which preserves only the original alignment, but others are well worth exploring – Watling Street around Affetside, a good example of a Roman ridgeway, and the section still to be described north of this. Such stretches offer the advantage of ready access, but usually cannot compete in interest with parts which are free of later roadways and yet preserve their original Roman features. Practically all our road from Ribchester north to Brougham, is of course in this category. In the section just concluded glimpses are afforded north of Starling, where a public path gives access. The footpaths, with right of way, from Radcliffe to Withins Reservoir, and north of this, from Doffer Fold to Higher Spen Moor, are approximately on the line, and may owe their origin to it, but there is little to see nowadays.

3. Over the moor

(Landranger 109, 103; Pathfinder 700, 689)

The straight stretch known as Watling Street, at its northern end, makes an oblique junction with the B6213, which itself immediately afterwards arrives at the A676 main road, almost opposite the Bull's Head. From this point the Roman road is thought (certainly by the Helmshore Local History Society, which studied this area in 1955) to follow the minor road which leaves the A676 in a north-westerly direction just east of the inn, following the contour and curving round the edge of the Waives Reservoir. In about a quarter of a mile this road (having straightened out and passed a minor cross-roads) bends towards the north-east at a point (744154) where a lane leaves it to the north-west (for Turton Bottoms). Close attention to the Pathfinder map is required here. Excavation by the Helmshore Society verified that the Roman road ran straight ahead between road and lane; a section was dug a short distance north of the junction, though no traces of the road are visible now (Aspin, 1955).

The Roman line is then thought to continue straight ahead, slightly west of north, parallel to the road to Edgworth and about 200 yards west of it. This would be a short linking alignment, pointing a little north of the main alignment, perhaps one of several to ease its passage across this rather difficult stretch of terrain. The present road comes back on to the main alignment in the vicinity of Wayoh Bridge, about a mile north-west of Edgworth, and the sharp bends by which this road then negotiates the steep gradients on each side of Broadhead Brook may well be original.

North of Wayoh Farm another short, straight, linking alignment – this time pointing further west – takes the present road, and the Roman line,

Figure 45: Looking north from south of Wayoh Bridge; the road zigzags up the steep opposite side of the valley to rejoin its alignment at the top; a feature which looks typically Roman.

to Pike House, where the main alignment is rejoined, although the present road continues to bend somewhat until after passing Grimeshill Bridge, about a quarter of a mile to the north. These local deviations may be occasioned, once again, by the crossing of the very deep and steep-sided gully at Grimeshill; certainly the winding approach, through cuttings, seems a typical piece of Roman engineering

The road is now approaching, at Rushton Heights, its highest point since leaving Manchester. Despite the local variations, especially in negotiating the difficult conditions of the last few miles, the road keeps returning to its original line, and it is evident that it was planned on a single alignment between its starting point near *Mancunium* and this high point at Rushton Heights. It is equally evident that Rushton Heights was a sighting point in laying out the road, for a slight change of alignment more to the north was made here. This was continued to the next sighting point, Jeffrey Hill, 13 miles to the north and clearly visible from here on a fine day.

The stretch of road we are following, north of Grimeshill, has other features of interest worth mentioning. Codrington noticed narrow enclosed strips of land running alongside it, some of which may still be seen. This is a feature often met with along Roman roads which have remained in use. According to Margary such roads often originally ran along a cleared road zone, with lines of demarcation set well back on each side. This resulted in wide verges which sometimes still remain (and are a sign of the road's antiquity); elsewhere, as here, the verges have in the course of time become fenced in as narrow strips. These often tend to push the road out of its original straight course, so that it gives the impression of winding a little though the map shows it to be very direct; Codrington remarks on this feature also in this stretch (Codrington, 1918).

The present road continues to follow the Roman line on through Blacksnape, now running on the hillside above Darwen, with wide views

Figure 46: From the hillside south of Grimeshill Bridge looking north at the steep descent into the gully of the stream; note the cuttings, the bends to ease the descent, and the resumption of the line on the opposite ridge.

across the town on the west. Codrington noted a parish boundary following the road for a quarter of a mile north of Blacksnape, but this is not now marked on the O.S. maps. At the Darwen-Hoddlesdon crossroads the present road swerves to the west towards Pot House, but there is no reason to think that the Roman road left the alignment; indeed Margary mentions the ridge on the eastern side of the present road in the first field north of the crossroads (Margary, 1957). The present road comes back on to the line about a mile and a quarter further north, bending sharply to the north-west at the point where a road to Hoddlesden branches off to the south-east. Actually, for about a quarter of a mile south of this point the line is continued by a fence, with signs of the ridge on its western side and accompanied by a footpath.

The present road then follows the Roman alignment for nearly two miles, until the outskirts of Blackburn are reached. It bends sharply on each side of Davy Field Bridge – bends which are likely to be part of the original course since a deep and steep-sided valley is crossed here. Close to this point a major new road was being constructed across the Roman line at the time of writing; one wonders if any traces of the old road have come to light. Further north the road, now called Roman Road on the street signs, widens out in passing through a modern industrial estate, after which it crosses the Darwen/Guide road and in about three-quarters of a mile, at Whinney Heights, it commences to bend to the west away from the Roman line in its final approach to Blackburn.

The Roman road does not seem to have determined the direction of any street within the present town of Blackburn (with the possible exception of parts of Shear Brow – see below), nor do older maps reveal any signs, but when definite traces are next met with beyond Ramsgreave, north of the town and three-and-a-half miles north of Whinney Heights, the alignment is exactly the same, and the presumption must be that this was maintained across the site of the town. This line would have crossed the Revidge road, in the northern part of the town, just west of Four Lane Ends, and in fact Codrington writes that in 1839 the ridge could be seen boldly approaching Revidge from the south (where East Park now extends) and was visible also north of Revidge road (Codrington, 1918).

Note on access
Most of the road length described in this section has been followed by present minor roads, interesting because they themselves have evidently been in use for centuries and are now, in their turn, being superseded by modern main roads. In fact it seems from the map that the Roman road north from Starling was the principal north/south route in this part of Lancashire, and that the major deviations from the Roman line were caused by the "pull" of Walshaw to the east and Darwen to the west. North of Blackburn modern roads – even minor ones – follow the Roman line very rarely until Penrith is reached; this is undoubtedly due, at least in part, to the mountainous nature of the route.

4. The approach to the Ribble

(Landranger 103; Pathfinder 689, 680)

As indicated in the last section, the road which climbs northwards out of Blackburn, Shear Brow, is perhaps worthy of mention in connexion with the Roman road we are following. The first (southern) section of this road is called Limbrick, and both names convey an impression of age. Certainly the road is by no means straight, nor does it coincide for any notable length with the Roman alignment, but the general direction is correct, and the hill climbed is so extremely steep that bends to ease the gradient would be very understandable. Shear Brow ends northwards at Four Lane Ends, and not far north of here a footpath which crosses the A6119 runs very close to the line.

However the first certain indication of the Roman road is the lane which runs north-westwards from Higher Ramsgreave Road, starting at 672312, a short distance east of Longworth's Farm (not the footpath running north at the farm itself). Looking back across Higher Ramsgreave Road from the start of this lane, the Roman line is seen continued southwards by a field boundary for some distance. For the first few yards of its course north from Higher Ramsgreave Road the lane is accompanied by a low ridge on its eastern side which may well mark the *agger*.

The map shows this lane to be exactly in line with the Roman road south of Blackburn (and with further indications ahead); it is roughly metalled and about 14 to 15 feet broad between the hedges. It maintains its straight course for about two-fifths of a mile, descending quite steeply; (on a clear day a stretch of road on exactly the same line can be seen northwards across the Ribble valley climbing Longridge Fell). Thereafter the

Figure 47: The lane which follows the Roman line northwards from Higher Ramsgreave Road, looking north.

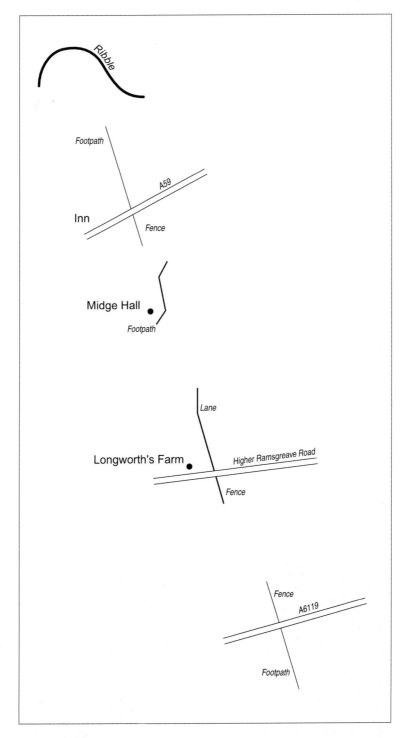

Sketch Map 15: The Roman Road from Blackburn to the Ribble (not to scale). The course of the road is marked at intervals by fences, lanes and footpaths.

lane bends eastwards not far from Midge Hall, before ending a short distance further on.

Evident traces of the road are now lost for about three-quarters of a mile until, not far short of the Longsight Road (A59), a field wall resumes the Roman line. This crosses the A59 in a north-westerly direction at a point (664332) about 200 yards east of the inn which stands opposite the end of Showley Road. From this point the Roman alignment is clearly marked by footpaths and field boundaries for the next mile, in fact to within a few hundred yards of the Ribble, which may well have changed its course somewhat since Roman times. Being perfectly straight and accompanied throughout by a right of way, the course of the Roman road is readily identified on the Pathfinder map.

The track northwards from the A59 (which continues a field boundary south of the A59 on the same line) commences as a pathway formerly maintained and macadamised, but it soon becomes a rough lane with an overgrown hedge on its eastern side. There are signs of the ridge, which become more prominent in the next field to the north; here the ridge is one/two feet high and two/three yards west of the same overgrown hedge, continuing in the same straight line. After crossing several fields the track arrives at a deep gully and sunken stream, immediately north of which, on the line of the road, is a derelict farmhouse (at 662337) marked with the sign JC 1871 and named as Stubbyhead House on older maps. North of this the line is resumed by a wet, sunken lane, again with an overgrown hedge on its eastern side, and then emerges into the open field, across which the ridge is still traceable. Further north, it again becomes enclosed when the lane to Catterall follows it for a short distance; this soon swerves off left (northwest) to Catterall, and the Roman line is continued by a field boundary, still accompanied by a right of way, straight ahead, for about 300 yards.

Figure 48: Looking north at the start (southern end) of the track which initially marks the line of the Roman road north of the A59, later continued by a hedge.

At the end of this stretch (659345) another track leads off east, but the track we have been following commences to descend to the flood-plain of the Ribble, following the gully of a small stream heading in the same general direction. The track winds somewhat in following this stream; it is highly probable that for some distance it still follows the Roman line, for the general direction is still very close to the main alignment and the descent very convenient, probably saving a good deal of construction work in grading etc. However, in its present form, this track bends along the river bank to give eventual access to a farm on the riverside some distance to the west; it is probable that it leaves the Roman line when the level flood-plain is reached; the Roman road must have continued on its north-west line to an adjacent ford. The very active River Ribble, which has washed away a substantial part of the Roman fort half a mile away, will very likely have obscured the actual crossing point, but the first certain stretch north of the river – Stonygate Lane, less than two miles away – is in exact alignment with the straight track which we have followed since the crossing of the A59.

Note on access

The lane running north from Higher Ramsgreave Road, though not marked as a right of way on the O.S. maps, shows all the signs of a bridleway. The track northwards from the A59 is a right of way throughout its length to the riverside, though the most northerly section, as indicated in the text, is not on the Roman alignment previously followed.

Bibliography

Abbreviations:

CW1 : Transactions of the Cumberland and Westmorland Antiquarian and
  Archaeological Society, 1st Series
CW2 : do., 2nd Series
L&CAS : Transactions of the Lancashire and Cheshire Antiquarian Society
MLPS : Transactions of the Manchester Literary and Philosophical Society

Allan, 1984 : Allan T.M., Note in *CW2 Newsletter no. 4, 1984.*
Anstee, 1975 : Anstee J.W., An Aqueduct in the Tebay Gorge, *Contrebis* III,
  74–75
Aspin, 1955 : Aspin C., The Roman Road near Edgeworth, *L&CAS* 65, 132
Austen, 1991 : Austen P.S., *Bewcastle and Old Penrith: A Roman Outpost Fort
  and a frontier Vicus*, Kendal
Birley, 1946 : Birley, E.B., The Roman Site at Burrow-in-Lonsdale, *CW2*
  XLVI, 126–156
Birley, 1947 : Birley, E.B., The Roman Fort at Low Borrow Bridge, *CW2*
  XLVII, 1–19
Birley, 1953 : Birley E. B., The Roman Milestone at Middleton in Lonsdale,
  CW2 LIII, 52–63
Charlesworth, 1965 : Charlesworth D., A Roman Milestone near Overtown,
  Lancs, *CW2* LXV, 427
Codrington, 1918 : Codrington T., *Roman Roads in Britain*, (3rd Edition)
  London, 98–110
Collingwood, 1933 : Collingwood R.G., Prehistoric Settlements near Crosby
  Ravensworth, *CW2* XXX111, 204–206
David and Charles, 1970 : *Reprints of the first edition of the one-inch Ordnance
  Survey of England and Wales (sheets 11,15 and 20),* Newton Abbott
Ekwall, 1971 : *The Concise Oxford Dictionary of English Place-Names* (4th edn.),
  Oxford
Ewbank, 1960 : Ewbank J. M., Cross-section of the Roman Road in Casterton,
  Westmorland, *CW2* LX, 28–31
Graystone, 1992 : Graystone P., *Walking Roman Roads in Bowland*, Lancaster
Higham and Jones, 1985 : Higham N.J. and Jones G.D.B., *The Carvetii*,
  Gloucester
Jones, 1974: Jones G. D. B., *Roman Manchester,* Altrincham
Just, 1842 : Just J., Note in *MLPS*, Vol. V11, (2nd series, p.3)
Lambert, 1996 : Lambert J (Ed), *Transect Through Time*, Lancaster
Leather, 1972 : Leather G.M., *Roman Lancaster*, Preston, RR/705a/1;
  RR/705b/1
Lowndes, 1963: Lowndes R.A.C., 'Celtic' Fields, farms and burial mounds in
  the Lune Valley, *CW2* LXIII, 77–95
Lowndes, 1964: Lowndes R.A.C., Excavation of a Romano-British Farmstead at
  Eller Beck, *CW2* LXIV, 1–13
Macadam, 1964: Macadam E.M.L., A Section of the Roman Road south of
  Low Borrow Bridge, Westmorland, *CW2* LXIV, 76–80

Margary, 1957: Margary I. D., *Roman Roads in Britain* (3rd Impression), London; Vol. 2

Ross, 1916 : Ross P., The Roman Road from Ribchester to Low Borrow Bridge (near Tebay), *Bradford Antiquary* VI, 243–66

Ross, 1920 : Ross P., The Roman Road north of Low Borrow Bridge to Brougham Castle, Westmorland, *CW2* XX, 1–15

Shotter, 1992 : Shotter D.C.A., The Roman Conquest of the North-West, in *Walking Roman Roads in Bowland* (P. Graystone) Lancaster, 1–5

Shotter & White, 1995 : Shotter D.C.A. and White A., *The Romans in Lunesdale*, Lancaster

Villy, 1937 : Villy F., The Roman Road north-west from Overborough, *CW2* XXXV11, 49

Watkin, 1883 : Watkin W.T., *Roman Lancashire*, Liverpool

Wilson 1883, Wilson T., The Roman Road over Whinfell, *CW1* V11, 90–95

Epilogue

Roman Carlisle

David Shotter

In this, the last of Philip Graystone's studies of Roman roads in north-west England, Carlisle, arguably the most significant Roman/Romano-British site in the region, is reached. Since archaeological research has, over the last 30 years, enlightened us a great deal regarding the nature, development and chronology of Roman Carlisle, it seems appropriate to conclude the present volume with a brief account of the site.

Carlisle – Roman *Luguvalium* – has long been 'the Border City': it is a description which is as appropriate to its Roman past as it is to later phases of the City's history. Its roles as a pivotal site for the Flavian advance into Scotland, for the Stanegate-*limes,* for Hadrian's Wall and, later, as the *civitas*-capital of the tribe of the Carvetii all serve to demonstrate this. The nature and extent of these roles, however, has become more fully apparent only since the 1970s, as large-scale urban development has afforded important archaeological opportunities, although the volume and quality of artefactual material recovered during the nineteenth and early-twentieth centuries had already pointed very clearly towards a site of considerable importance (McCarthy, 1999). Nor has such evidence come from Carlisle alone: writing-tablets from the rich collection recovered from Vindolanda have also hinted at Carlisle's significance in the organisation and administration of the frontier-zone (Birley, Birley and Birley, 1993).

Roman Carlisle was approached initially along the line of the present A6-road (Botchergate); it is clear that, in common with other Roman fort-sites in the north, the military establishment was founded not simply on cleared woodland, but on land that was already under arable cultivation (McCarthy, 1993,2; Wilmott, 1997,39; Huntley, 1999,54). Little in detail was known of the fort, until excavations took place in the 1970s and 1980s on sites in the area of Annetwell Street. Here, elements of the fort's south gateway and southern ramparts were uncovered, revealing an extraordinary level of preservation of organic and metallic material; the survival of the turves of the rampart itself and of the timbers of the gateway and adjacent guard-towers displayed substantial portions of the kind of arrangement which is best seen in the well-known reconstructions at the Lunt (Coventry).

The recovery of such material from these sites indicated beyond doubt that, since these represented the southern boundary of the fort, the bulk of the fort's remains lay beneath the Castle and Castle Green (on the opposite side of the modern ring-road). This has most recently been confirmed in excavations conducted by Carlisle Archaeology Ltd. (1999-2001) on the Castle Green. Inside the fort, surviving features have been the main road leading towards the headquarters building *(principia)*, parts of the headquarters building itself, workshops *(fabricae)* and many phases of barrack-buildings; amongst the details that have been revealed have been the timber-lined drains which flanked the main road inside the fort and, in the gateway itself, a timber threshold so deeply rutted by the wheels of vehicles that it had required replacement.

Important as such details were, however, the most significant result of these excavations has been the establishment, through the dating-technique of dendrochronology (tree-ring analysis of surviving timbers), that the timbers used in the original construction of the fort had by and large been felled in the autumn of A.D.72. This was, as a result, one of the first Roman forts in the north-west where it was established beyond doubt that, contrary to general opinion at the time, the governor, Gnaeus Julius Agricola (A.D.77–83), had *not* been responsible for the foundation. Carlisle had clearly been established by Quintus Petillius Cerialis (governor, A.D.71–74), as he continued the work of his predecessor, Marcus Vettius Bolanus (governor, A.D.69–71), in establishing Roman control amongst the Brigantes and the Carvetii following the 'revolt of Venutius' in 69 (Tacitus, *Histories* III.45; Birley, R., 1973; Shotter, 2000a and b; 2001a; 2002, forthcoming).

At the time of the Roman invasion of Britain in A.D.43, the emperor, Claudius, had 'bought' peace in the north through a 'deal' with Cartimandua, the 'queen' of the Brigantes (Richmond, 1954; Shotter, 1994), whose principal centre was probably the large and developing *oppidum* at Stanwick, at the eastern entrance to the Stainmore Pass (Turnbull, 1984). A major feature of this 'deal' was that the pro-Roman queen should marry Venutius, who was probably the chief of the Carvetii (Higham and Jones, 1985), and who probably had his centre at the western entrance to the Stainmore Pass at Clifton Dykes (near Brougham); Venutius' enthusiasm for Rome was clearly a great deal less intense than was that of his new wife. In A.D.69, Venutius had broken his agreement with Rome, expelled Cartimandua from Stanwick and effectively taken control of northern England. As the Roman historian, Cornelius Tacitus, put it, 'Venutius got a kingdom: we were left with a war to fight'.

In such a situation, it is clear that a developing network of communications was of crucial importance; troops were barracked in the north Midlands at sites such as Wroxeter and Little Chester (Derby), from where they could be marched northwards, along 'King Street', towards Lancaster and the Lune and Eden valleys. Further troops were probably transported from the Dee estuary, up the coast of north-west England, as far north perhaps as Solway; detachments of such troops, probably the 'marine legionaries' of legion II *Adiutrix,* could be disembarked in the north-west's broad estuaries. At the same time, further troops marched up on the eastern side of the Pennines; communications between them and their 'western colleagues' will have been of great importance; probably the most significant of these 'linking routes' will have been that which passed over

Stainmore to meet the main northward route (described in this volume) at Brougham.

The fort at Carlisle initially housed a garrison of cavalry; it emerges from a writing-tablet discovered at Carlisle (Tomlin, 1998) that this was the *Ala Gallorum Sebosiana,* a unit perhaps associated with legion II *Adintrix,* and which was later to be garrisoned at Lancaster (Shotter, 2001b). From this unit, the tablet indicates, Agricola, as governor, chose men to form his official bodyguard (*equites singulares*).

After A.D.78, the chief emphasis of Agricola's military activity was in Scotland (Hanson, 1987), culminating in 83 with his 'genocidal' victory over the Caledonians at the still-elusive site of *Mons Graupius* (Maxwell,1990). We should remember, however, that this northward progress will not have rendered the fort at Carlisle redundant; far from it. There was the work of consolidation to be continued in north-west England; early modifications at the fort at Carlisle itself, together with other newly-recognised military sites in the area (McCarthy,1999), suggest that Carlisle and its hinterland were probably used as winter-quarters for troops fighting further north (Caruana,1992; Tomlin,1992). In this connection, the outstanding finds of armour made in the most recent excavations on Castle Green (2000–01) may be relevant.

In c.A.D.87, largely because of growing pressures elsewhere in the empire, the decision was taken to abandon the recent conquests in much of Scotland and to develop a frontier-zone centred on the road which ran between Corbridge and Carlisle and which, since medieval times, has been known as 'the Stanegate' (Graystone,1994; Hodgson, 2000; Jones, 1990). As the Stanegate was developed to the west of Carlisle, through Solway, to Kirkbride (possibly *Briga* of the Vindolanda-tablets), so the role of Carlisle itself may also have developed. The recently-discovered fort at Cummersdale (some three miles south-west of Carlisle) suggests that the extended Stanegate may have formally 'bypassed' Carlisle, leaving the site, as some of the Vindolanda-tablets seem to suggest, with a role that was more regional than purely local. The road which had been established perhaps as early as the governorship of Petillius Cerialis running from Carlisle, through Blennerhasset (Evans and Scull,1990) to the coast at Maryport or Beckfoot, perhaps foreshadowed such a regional role.

It is clear, however, that by the late-first or early-second century the fort-commander at Carlisle evidently exercised a responsibility at least as far east as Vindolanda; indeed, an interesting recent discovery which has served to point this up has been that of a previously unknown bath-house constructed outside the south gate of the fort at Vindolanda very early in the second century; a writing-tablet from Vindolanda indicates that this work was facilitated by the commander at Carlisle.

In the first two decades of the second century, Carlisle may again have seen 'front-line action': we are told that, when Hadrian became emperor in A.D.117, 'the Britons could no longer be held under Roman control'. Although details are lacking, it seems increasingly likely that the 'troubles' were centred in the west of the frontier-zone. The Romans were evidently victorious by 119, but changes were signalled; in the aftermath, orders appear to have been sent from Rome to 'beef up' the frontier by the construction of a turf wall to run from the Irthing-crossing at Willowford to Bowness-on-Solway. On this occasion, the actual frontier-line appears to have by-passed Carlisle to the north, with the establishment of a new fort at Stanwix; the commanding role which evidently attached to this new fort serves to underline the continuing importance of Carlisle in regional organisation – an importance which will *not* have diminished against the background of changing frontier-policy during the remainder of the second century.

In A.D.122, Hadrian himself visited Britain, and modified the plans for the frontier; he ordered stone to be used for the construction instead of turf and a new start to the building to be made from Newcastle (*Pons Aelius*). The modification in building-materials seems to have led eventually, but in any case by the end of Hadrian's reign in A.D.138, to the rebuilding in stone of the original turf elements in the west. As before, Carlisle's role was probably principally one of regional organisation, and there was evidence in the recent excavations on Castle Green of rebuilding-work in the centre of the fort by men of legion VI *Victrix,* which had been brought to Britain by Hadrian in 122, and based in the fortress at York.

As usually happened outside Roman forts, civilian activity developed early on, as people came and settled to offer a range of goods and services for which a military garrison and its men would pay good money; the range and numbers of soldiers involved in Carlisle and in its immediate hinterland will have guaranteed that such opportunities were especially favourable. A number of widely-separated sites in Carlisle have yielded evidence of civilian activity. Immediately outside the fort (on Castle Street; McCarthy, 1991), there was strong evidence of industrial processes, including the working of leather. So close to the fort, this was probably undertaken by civilians, but under military supervision.

Conventional 'strip-buildings' have been located at Blackfriars Street (McCarthy, 1990); such structures are well-known in extramural settlements, consisting of a long, narrow building with its gable-end facing the street-frontage, and a range of living- and working-space behind. This building continued in use throughout the Roman period – and, as we shall see, beyond. Further 'strip-buildings' have been located, fronting on to Botchergate (the main street leading to the south gate of the fort); here, too, industrial activity appears to have been important. A larger area of civilian activity has been located in the area of 'The Lanes' (McCarthy, 2000) – a series of medieval streets, which overlie 'alleys' of Roman date which separated properties into 'blocks' (*insulae).* This area lies between the modern Scotch Street/English Street and Lowther Street. Again, there is evidence of industrial activity, and at least one substantial 'courtyard-building', of which one room was equipped with central heating; perhaps it belonged to an official, or to a successful entrepreneur. If Carlisle developed in any way similarly to Corbridge, then we should expect there to have been extensive mercantile and industrial activity (cf. Bishop and Dore, 1988).

As we have seen, the soldiers themselves in the fort can be expected to have had a range of needs – personal, social, religious and leisure-based; all will have been catered for either officially or by businesses established in the extramural settlement. People manufactured items, sold on goods purchased from travelling salesmen, and acted as 'middlemen' for farmers from Carlisle's hinterland – using or selling their crops, slaughtering their beasts and selling the meat, or processing the 'by-products'. The more vibrant and extensive the military market became, the more civilians will have been attracted to take advantage of it, thus swelling the potential market for goods and services even more. In the process, Carlisle, like other similar sites, will have become a truly cosmopolitan place – with people of local origin mixing with retired soldiers and immigrants from various parts of the empire. In no area will such a diverse population have been more noticeable than in the field of religion; the diversity will have encouraged a range of polytheistic pagan cults (including tutelary deities of Carlisle itself and of its region, which helped to concentrate people's attention on to the Romanised way of life), of eastern 'mystery-cults' (such as Mithraism) and, in time, Christianity itself, which is represented on the tombstone of the Greek, Flavius Antigonus Papias, who died when he was 'sixty years old, *more or less'*. As such a population mixed together, sharing a rich variety of cultural experiences, all will have become part of the process of Romanisation or, as the historian, Dio Cassius (56.18,2), put it, 'becoming different without knowing it'.

As we saw earlier, Hadrian visited Britain in A.D.122; although he was principally concerned with military matters, he evidently also found time to look to civilian affairs. Almost certainly it was he who devolved some local administrative responsibility to the eastern Brigantes, centred upon the town (*civitas*-capital) of Aldborough (*Isurium Brigantum*) in Yorkshire (Hartley and Fitts, 1988). Perhaps about a century later, another such privilege was given – on this occasion, to the Carvetii of north-west England, the tribe of Venutius. This 'promotion' is demonstrated by the inscription on a milestone which was found near Brougham, and which dates to the reign of the rebel-emperor, Postumus (A.D.259–268; see *Journal of Roman Studies* 55 (1965), 224). Carlisle was chosen as the *civitas*-capital, presumably because of its long-standing regional role and because of the size of its extramural settlement. The granting of this privilege also demonstrates that the local leaders of the Carvetii, many of whom were presumably farmers in Solway and in the Eden valley, were loyal, wealthy and enjoyed the capacity for continued wealth-generation: leaders of local government had to be able to pay for their privileges on a long-term basis.

That this 'promotion' will have brought with it the physical development of the necessary buildings of high status – (for example, a *forum*) – is in little doubt, although direct evidence of this is limited in extent. It is thought, however, that the demolition of 'strip-buildings' on Botchergate in the early-third century and the reversion of that part of the site to use as a cemetery-area may provide an indication of major replanning in the town. Further, excavations in the Lanes-area revealed fragments of monumental buildings consonant with an elevation of Carlisle's status. The clear and significant implication of this is that for the final century-and-a-half of the Roman occupation much of northern England enjoyed a measure of self-administration. However, it should be added that the continuing evidence of military activity of some kind suggests that local leaders may have shared their responsibility with the Roman army.

Little is known in detail of the later years of Roman Carlisle, although excavations at the fort of Birdoswald (Wilmott, 1997; 2001) suggest that the overarching military organisation in the frontier-zone may have been loosening, with more responsibility falling on to the shoulders of local leaders. Some sites, at least, appear to have been taking on the character of strong-points where a local militia looked after and defended its community in an increasingly independent atmosphere.

We should not, however, take this as an indication of eagerness on the part of Carvetian leaders to cast aside the Roman 'yoke'. On the contrary, certain sites in Carlisle have provided clear signs that the opposite was the case – that the Romano-British of the Carvetii were anxious to defend what they regarded as their culture (cf.Johnson, 1980). Dating-evidence from the 'strip-house' on Blackfriars Street, for example, indicates not only that it was rebuilt in a substantial style in the later-fourth century, but that it must have survived in this form well into the fifth; indeed, it is apparent that the integrity of its 'building-line' was respected until as late as the seventh century. Further, a bath-house uncovered beneath St Alban's Church (on Scotch Street; McCarthy, Keevil and Shotter, 1989) also showed signs of very late rebuilding, and thus continued in use well into the fifth century.

Nor should it be overlooked that, in his *Life of St Cuthbert* (27), Bede indicates that, on a visit to Carlisle in A.D.685, Cuthbert was shown a water-fountain (and thus, by implication, a working aqueduct) of the Roman period; his 'guide' was a man who evidently still used Roman titles (*praepositus* of the *urbs*). Descendants of the Romanised Carvetian leadership must still in the seventh century have been able to maintain intact parts, at least, of the material culture of their forebears. At the end of the day, Romanisation was clearly a great deal more than 'skin-deep' in *Luguvalium;* we can be certain that in Carlisle, as elsewhere, it was only slowly that the Romano-British once again 'became different without knowing it'.

References (for Epilogue)

Bidwell, 1999: Bidwell P.T.(Ed), *Hadrian's Wall, 1989–1999,* Kendal

Birley A.R.,1973: Birley A.R., Petillius Cerialis and the Conquest of Brigantia, *Britannia* 4, 179–190

Birley, Birley and Birley, 1993: Birley E.B., Birley R. and Birley A.R., *Vindolanda II: The Early Wooden Forts,* Hexham

Bishop and Dore, 1988: Bishop M.C. and Dore J.N., *Corbridge: Excavations of the Roman Fort and Town, 1947–80,* London

Caruana, 1992: Caruana I.D, Carlisle: Excavation of a section of the annexe-ditch of the first Flavian Fort, 1990, *Britannia* 23, 45–109

Evans and Scull, 1990: Evans J. and Scull C., Fieldwork on the Roman Fort Site at Blennerhasset, Cumbria, *CW 2* 90, 127–138

Graystone, 1994: Graystone P., *Walking Roman Roads in East Cumbria,* Lancaster

Hanson, 1987: Hanson W.S., *Agricola and the Conquest of the North,* London

Hartley and Fitts, 1988: Hartley B.R. and Fitts L., *The Brigantes,* Stroud

Higham and Jones, 1985: Higham N.J. and Jones G.D.B., *The Carvetii,* Stroud

Hodgson, 2000: Hodgson N., The Stanegate: A Frontier Rehabilitated, *Britannia* 31, 11–22

Huntley, 1999: Huntley J.P., Environmental Evidence from Hadrian's Wall, pp.49–64 in Bidwell, 1999

Johnson, 1980: Johnson A.S., *Later Roman Britain,* London

Jones, 1990: Jones G.D.B., The Emergence of the Tyne-Solway Frontier, pp.98–107 in Maxfield V.A.and Dobson M. J. (Eds), *Roman Frontier Studies, 1989,* Exeter

Maxwell, 1990: Maxwell G.S., *A Battle Lost,* Edinburgh

McCarthy, 1990: McCarthy M.R., *A Roman, Anglian and Medieval Site at Blackfriars Street, Carlisle: Excavations 1977–9,* Kendal

McCarthy, 1991: McCarthy M.R., *The Roman Waterlogged Remains and Later Features at Castle Street, Carlisle: Excavations 1981–2,* Kendal

McCarthy, 1993: McCarthy M.R., *Carlisle: History and Guide,* Stroud.
McCarthy, 1999: McCarthy M.R., *Carlisle – Luguvalium,* pp.168–177 in Bidwell, 1999

McCarthy, 2000: McCarthy M.R, *Roman and Medieval Carlisle; The Southern Lanes,* Carlisle

McCarthy, Keevil and Shotter, 1989: McCarthy M.R, Keevil G.D. and Shotter D.C.A., A Gold *Solidus* of Valentinian II from Scotch Street, Carlisle, *Britannia* 20, 254–255

Richmond, 1954: Richmond I.A., Queen Cartimandua, *Journ. Rom. Studies* 44, 43–52

Shotter, 1994: Shotter D.C.A., Rome and the Brigantes: Early Hostilities, *CW 2* 94, 21–34

Shotter, 2000a: Shotter D.C.A., Petillius Cerialis in Northern Britain, *Northern History* 36, 189–198

Shotter, 2000b: Shotter D.C.A., The Roman Conquest of the North-West, *CW* 2 100, 33–53

Shotter, 2001a: Shotter D.C.A., Petillius Cerialis in Carlisle: a Numismatic Contribution, *CW* 3 1, 21–30

Shotter, 2001b: Shotter D.C.A., Roman Lancaster: Site and Settlement, pp.3–31 in White A.J.(Ed), *A History of Lancaster,* Edinburgh

Shotter, 2002: Shotter D.C.A., Roman Britain and the Year of the Four Emperors, *CW* 3 2 (forthcoming)

Tomlin, 1992: Tomlin R.S.O., The Twentieth Legion at Wroxeter and Carlisle in the first century: The Epigraphic Evidence, *Britannia* 23, 141–158

Tomlin, 1998: Tomlin R.S.O., Roman Manuscripts from Carlisle: The Ink-written Tablets, *Britannia* 29, 31–84

Turnbull, 1984: Turnbull P., Stanwick in the Northern Iron Age, *Durham Arch. Journ.* 1, 41–49

Wilmott, 1997: Wilmott T., *Birdoswald, Excavations of a Roman Fort on Hadrian's Wall, 1987–92,* London

Wilmott, 2001: Wilmott T., *Birdoswald Roman Fort: 1800 Years on Hadrian's Wall,* Stroud

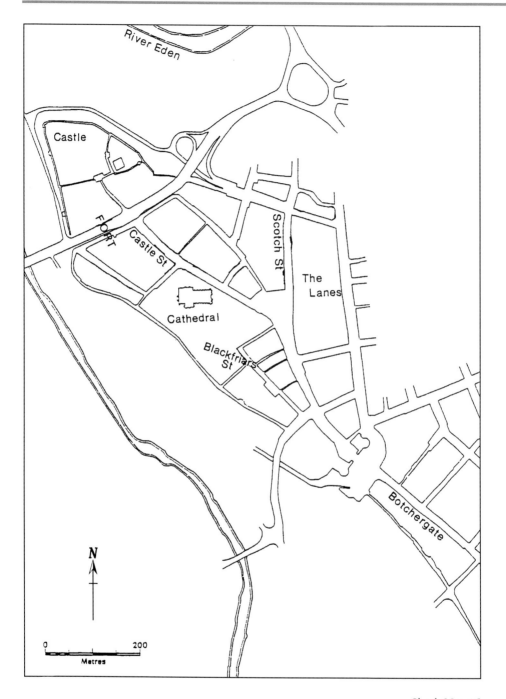

Sketch Map 16: Carlisle: sites mentioned in the text.

Index

Notes on the Index

1) This index, of proper names and road numbers, covers the main text of the book, from page 1 to page 74, and from page 77 to page 83 inclusive. It does not cover the introductory material (pages I to XII) nor the pages of references (pages 75 to 76, 83 to 85). Nor does it cover the page headings, except those at the beginning of each section.

2) The names of authors referred to as sources in the text will not be found in this index, since they are listed alphabetically in the pages of references detailed above.

A58 59, 60
A59 67, 68, 69
A6 36, 37, 38, 39, 72
A6119 66, 67
A65 2, 4, 5, 48
A66 35
A665 59
A676 63
A683 7, 8, 9, 10, 11, 12, 43
A684 13
A685 19, 50, 51
Aelia Sentica 19
Affetside (Cross) 61, 62
Agricola (Gnaeus Julius) 73, 74
Ala Gallorum Sebosiana 74
Aldborough 76
Annetwell Street 72
Aqueduct (Tebay) 19, 20, 21
Artle Beck 42, 43
Artle Mill 44
Aurelius Verulus 19

B6196 60
B6213 63
B6257 13
B6261 24, 25, 26, 27
B6262 33
B6292 59, 60
Barbon (Beck) 4, 6, 7, 8
Battle House 46
Beckfoot 74

Bede (St.) 77
Birdoswald 77
Birk Knott 19
Blackbeck Bridge 7, 9
Blackburn 65, 66, 67
Blackfriars Street 75, 77
Blacksnape 64, 65
Blea Beck 27, 28, 29, 31
Bleak House 36
Blennerhasset 74
Bolanus (Marcus Vettius) 73
Borrans (The) 52
Borrow Beck 50, 51
Borrowdale 53
Botchergate 37, 72, 75, 76
Bowness-on-Solway 75
Briga 74
Brigantes 73, 76
Brigflatts 12
Britain 75, 76
Britons 74
Broadhead Brook 63
Brougham 26, 32, 33, 34, 35, 36, 37, 62, 73, 74, 76
Broughton 59
Bruton F.A. 55
Bull's Head 63
Burrow Hall 43, 44
Burrow-in-Lonsdale 1, 5, 11, 17, 41, 43, 44, 45, 46, 57
Bury New Road 59, 62

Caledonians 74
Carlinghill (Bridge) 14, 19, 50
Carlingill Beck 13, 15, 16
Carlisle 1, 36, 37, 38, 39, 41, 57
   and *passim* 72 to 77
Carlton 38
Cartimandua 73
Carvetii 11, 34, 72, 73, 76, 77
Casterton 4, 5, 7
Castle Green 72, 73, 74, 75
Castlefield 55
Castle Street 75
Caton 43, 44
Catterall 68
Central Station 55
Cerialis (Quintus Petillius) 73, 74
Christianity 76
Claudius 73
Claughton 43
Clifton Dykes 73
Coalpit Hill 31
Cockin (Whinfell) 52
Cockin (Whittington) 45, 46, 49
Corbridge 74, 75
Cowan Bridge 1
Crosby Ravensworth 24, 26, 27, 28, 31
Crosby Ravensworth Fell 26
Cross Stone 6, 7, 8, 12
Crow Trees Farm 59

Occasional Papers from the Centre for North-West Regional Studies

The Centre for North-West Regional Studies, based at Lancaster University, brings together members of the university and the regional community. As well as its extensive publication programme of books and resource papers, it organises conferences, study days and seminars covering a wide range of subjects. For a small annual subscription 'Friends of the Centre' receive regular mailings of events and discounts on books and other activities.

For further details contact Centre for North-West Regional Studies, Fylde College, Lancaster University, Lancaster, LAI 4YF; tel: 01524 593770; fax: 01524 594725; email: christine.wilkinson@lancaster.ac.uk; Web site: www.lancs.ac.uk/users/cnwrs/

Walking Roman Roads in Lonsdale and the Eden Valley, 2002, Philip Graystone	£10.95
The Wray Flood of 1967, 2002, Emmeline Garnett	£10.95
A Fylde Country Practice, 2001, Steven King	£10.95
The Arts & Crafts Movement in the Lake District: A Social History, 2001, Jennie Brunton	£10.95
Irish Women in Lancashire, 2001, Sharon Lambert	£9.95
Hadrian's Wall: A Social and Cultural History, 2000, Alison Ewin	£8.50
Furness Abbey: Romance, Scholarship and Culture, 2000, C. Dade-Robertson	£11.50
Rural Industries of the Lune Valley, 2000, Michael Winstanley	£9.95
The Romans at Ribchester, 2000, B. J. N. Edwards	£8.95
The Buildings of Georgian Lancaster (revised edition), 2000, Andrew White	£6.95
A History of Linen in the North West, 1998, ed. Elizabeth Roberts	£6.95
History of Catholicism in the Furness Peninsula, 1998, Anne C. Parkinson	£6.95
Vikings in the North West – The Artifacts, 1998, B. J. N. Edwards	£6.95
Sharpe, Paley and Austin, A Lancaster Architectural Practice 1836–1952, 1998, James Price	£6.95
Victorian Terraced Housing in Lancaster, 1996, Andrew White and Mike Winstanley	£6.95
Walking Roman Roads in the Fylde and the Ribble Valley, 1996, Philip Graystone	£5.95
Romans in Lunesdale, 1995, David Shotter and Andrew White	£6.50
Roman Route Across the Northern Lake District, Brougham to Moresby, 1994, Martin Allan	£5.95
Walking Roman Roads in East Cumbria, 1994, Philip Graystone	£5.95
St Martin's College, Lancaster, 1964–89, 1993, Peter S. Gedge and Lois M. R. Louden	£5.95
From Lancaster to the Lakes: the Region in Literature, 1992, eds Keith Hanley and Alison Millbank	£5.95
Windermere in the Nineteenth Century, 1991, ed. Oliver M. Westall	£4.95
Grand Fashionable Nights: Kendal Theatre, 1989, Margaret Eddershaw	£3.95
Rural Life in South West Lancashire, 1988, Alistair Mutch	£3.95
The Diary of William Fisher of Barrow, 1986, eds William Rollinson and Brett Harrison	£2.95
Richard Marsden and the Preston Chartists, 1981, J. E. King	£2.95

Each of these titles may be ordered by post from the above address, postage and packing £1.00 per order. Please make cheques payable to 'The University of Lancaster'. Titles are also available from all good booksellers in the region.